Anderson's Social Philosophy

ANDERSON'S SOCIAL PHILOSOPHY

A.J. Baker

Angus & Robertson Publishers

Angus & Robertson Publishers
London · Sydney · Melbourne · Singapore · Manila

First published by Angus & Robertson Publishers, Australia, 1979

© A. J. Baker 1979

National Library of Australia
Cataloguing-in-publication data.

Baker, A. J.
  Anderson's social philosophy.

  Index.
  ISBN 0 207 13813 3 hardbound
  ISBN 0 207 14216 5 paperbound

  1. Anderson, John, 1893–1962.   2. Social sciences-Philosophy.
  I. Title.

300.1

Filmset in Hong Kong
by Asco Trade Typesetting Ltd
Printed in Hong Kong

CONTENTS

PREFACE

If few university men are really original thinkers, it is also true that few of them, original or not, are prepared to speak out in a bold and uncompromising way on controversial questions. But John Anderson, 1893–1962, combined each of these unusual characteristics. A philosopher with remarkably wide interests, ranging through social theory, ethics and aesthetics, as well as the main areas of "general" or "pure" philosophy, he is arguably the most original thinker in *each* of these areas that Australian philosophy has had. At the same time, though he was by profession an academic absolutely devoted to intellectual inquiry, he was no aloof theorist, shutting himself off from society and its conflicts; on the contrary, as a result of his willingness to comment critically on issues of the day, whether they concerned censorship, education, patriotism, politics or religion, he became Australia's foremost advocate of freedom of thought and of a critical, thinking approach to public questions.

Partly because of the very range of his intellectual interests, Anderson's thought is less well represented in print than we could wish. He had a striking impact on his many dedicated students, but this was as much through his lectures, addresses and contributions to discussion as it was through his written work on philosophy. He wrote no systematic treatise, and the one book presenting an overall view of his position, his *Studies in Empirical Philosophy*, although a valuable collection of many of his important articles, is not a single, unified study. If, however, his general philosophy has not been developed and defended as thoroughly as it might have been, the situation is far worse with his social thought. In this area, except for his rather better elaborated ethics—which is a vital ingredient in his social philosophy—his position appears in print only in numerous, but mainly fragmented, essays and critiques. This is a consequence of his active participation in social movements and struggles; his social and political publications were mostly written in response to occasional or polemical needs.

In this book, therefore, I concentrate on an exposition and elucidation of Anderson's social philosophy, rather than on possible criticisms, or disagreements of my own with his views. In so doing, I have approached the subject in two different but complementary ways. I deal in Part I with Anderson's *theory* and try to set out systematically the basic parts of his social position, including his ethics and his assessment of Marxism. Then I deal in Part II with his thinking in the historical context of his varying political allegiances and the public controversies in which he was involved. It is consequently in that part that I give an account of the *policies* he advocated, though it is there too that I give an outline of the early Communist theory which he later largely abandoned. It seemed better not to include questions about Anderson's influence and a retrospective look at his work in this book, so I merely say something about these in conclusion.

I am much indebted to Alice R. Walker for various helpful comments and for allowing me to see her notes of a number of lectures and addresses given by Anderson.

A.J. Baker

Abbreviations of Journals and Newspapers

A.J.P.	*The Australasian Journal of Philosophy*. Journal of the Australasian Association of Philosophy = A.A.P.
A.J.P.P.	*The Australasian Journal of Psychology and Philosophy*. Name of the A.J.P. before 1947 and Journal of the A.A.P.P.
A.H.	*The Australian Highway*. Journal of the Workers' Educational Association, Sydney.
D.T.	*The Daily Telegraph*, Sydney.
H.S.	*Honi Soit*, student newspaper, University of Sydney.
S.M.H.	*The Sydney Morning Herald*.
T.C.	*The Communist*. Theoretical organ of the Communist Party of Australia.
T.M.	*The Militant*. Journal of the Workers' Party (Left Opposition), Sydney.
U.R.	*The Union Recorder*, University of Sydney.
W.W.	*The Workers' Weekly*. Journal of the Communist Party of Australia.

Abbreviations of Frequently Cited Writings by Anderson

S   *Studies in Empirical Philosophy*, Angus & Robertson, Sydney, 1962.

AM   "Art and Morality", *A.J.P.P.*, December 1941, pp. 253–66.

DI   "Democratic Illusions", *Hermes*, Journal of the University of Sydney, 1952, pp. 16–18. (This issue did not appear until 1954.)

EP   *Education and Politics*, a collection of four essays, Angus & Robertson, Sydney, 1931.

FC   "Freedom and the Working Class", *Proletariat*, Journal of the Melbourne University Labour Club, No. 2, July 1932, pp. 2–6.

FT   "Freedom of Thought", *Freethought*, Journal of the Sydney University Freethought Society, No. 1, July 1932, pp. 1–3.

LS   "Leadership and Spontaneity", in a pamphlet, *Censorship in the Working Class Movement*, published by the Sydney University Freethought Society, October 1932, pp. 2–8.

OF   "Some Obscurantist Fallacies", *Freethought*, No. 2, November 1932, pp. 10–12.

PA   "The Place of the Academic in Modern Society", *Honi Soit*, 16 June 1960, p. 5.

PD   "Introductory Essay", *Prospects of Democracy*, ed. W.H.C. Eddy, Sydney, 1945, pp. 7–12.

PP   "The Politics of Proscription", *The Australian Quarterly*, June 1948, pp. 7–15.

RA   "Critical Notice of H.B. Acton, *The Illusion of the Epoch*", *A.J.P.*, August 1959, pp. 156–67.

RE   "Religion in Education", included in *Religion in Education* (five addresses) published by the New Education Fellowship, Sydney, 1943.

SS   "Social Service", *Freethought*, No. 3, May 1936, pp. 2–7.

TW   "The Working Class", *Proletariat*, No. 1, April 1932, pp. 3–6.

PART I: SOCIAL AND ETHICAL THEORY

PHILOSOPHY AND SOCIAL
SCIENCE

In Anderson's view there is no logical or theoretical distinction between social or historical sciences and any other field of investigation. All sciences, the human no less than those dealing with non-human material, are studies of definite types of occurrences or situations, in space and time. Similarly he felt that in all fields there are obstacles to objective study, including the complexity of the material studied and the constant presence of socio-mental forces or interests, both of which promote illusion. In a statement of the true philosophical, scientific and critical outlook, of which he takes the early Greek philosopher Heraclitus to be the great pioneer exhibitor, Anderson writes about

> ... the thorough-going objectivism of ... Heraclitus, who was unremitting in his attack on subjectivist illusions, on the operation of desire or the imagining of things as we should like them to be, as opposed to the operation of understanding or the finding of things (including our own activities) as they positively are, with no granting of a privileged position in reality to gods, men or molecules, with conflict everywhere and nothing above the battle. (S pp. 193–94)

But if every science has to struggle against confusions and be alive to "criticism of the categories" this is all the more evident in the social, psychological and ethical fields. In the development of science "the work of disentangling reality from fiction is all the harder ... the nearer the subject lies to the centre of our interests and the more it is played upon by our hopes and fears", and this is particularly the case with human affairs. (S p. 238) Barriers to progress, Anderson argues, are found in the evident deficiencies of most potential investigators in the social and political fields. On the one hand, he cuttingly observes, those people who are academically educated are all too often "saturated ... with respectability" and "are content to worship the idols of the market place". "And, since on the other hand, those who are immersed in social struggles have not for the most part had a scientific training, it is not difficult to understand why social science so conspicuously fails to progress." (SS p. 2)

In his terminology Anderson, like Karl Marx for example, makes no particular distinction between "social science", "historical science", "sociology" or "social philosophy"—except perhaps that, as does Marx, he uses, "social philosophy" to suggest a greater emphasis on *criticism*, on clearing away confusions and laying the foundations for intellectual progress. As an extension of this kind of approach he often spoke of "social theory" or "social criticism", using these more tentative-sounding terms to register the fact that there is a gap between potential and achievement: that while there is a genuine *subject*, the science of society, available for investigation and advance, the actual present day state of social *study* or *theory* is backward and confused. This is contrary to the more grandiose assumptions of American and other (and nowadays Australian) sociologists, and the allied class of self-proclaimed political *scientists*, so many of whose contentions involve pretensions and obfuscations that are vulnerable to critical examination. Certainly Anderson, as part of his unrelenting campaign "to expose illusions", rarely missed an opportunity to criticise, and indeed satirise, the unexamined "concepts" or "interpretations" and the superficial "empirical data" that are deployed in the use of social questionnaires and statistics, the making of election studies, social strata surveys, and so on.

In Anderson's view, then, there is a genuine science of society in the sense both that there is a complex of truths concerning social occurrences or activities which (1) are the case, and (2) are open to discovery; but with reference to the latter we have to understand that the activity of discovering these truths, the practice of social science, is itself a social occurrence subject to historical conditions, and its present position is of such a kind that it is a putative rather than an established, fully-fledged scientific discipline. In these circumstances, the inquirer must expend considerable effort in the formulation and clarification of issues, and more generally in establishing the *categories* or basic "concepts" of the social field. In so doing he must also criticise confused views that prevail in the field, in particular mistaken beliefs or assumptions about what the social categories are. The social inquirer, therefore, in the course of making positive contributions, also has an important negative role. He is, to begin with, presenting a preliminary survey of the science of society, and in so doing he must be a philosophical *critic*, one more of those necessary under-labourers clearing away the rubbish that lies in the path of knowledge. In so doing he can place his positive account of the categories on a firmer foundation and so facilitate the consequent main task of social science—that of presenting and confirming hypotheses about various forms and sets of social occurrences and their interrelations.

Justice cannot be done here to Anderson's central philosophical position, though some reference to it, including his general theory of the categories, needs to be made.[1] His position is, above all, one of realism, empiricism and pluralism. Stating these baldly, his *realism*, which criticises philosophical idealism in particular, asserts that when a mind knows something, there is a genuine relationship involved between the knower and the known, both of which are independently real things. The contrary supposition —that the known thing is "mind-dependent" or "constituted" by being known—involves a type of confusion which Anderson calls "relativism". Relativism is an illicit running together of questions about qualities and questions about relations, as is illustrated by the idealist view that in consciousness or experience the "object" of which we are conscious is *inseparable* from the conscious "subject". Against this view the realist points out that when A is conscious of B, A and B are each independent things with qualities of their own and the relation, A's being conscious of B, is a quite separate fact.

Anderson's *empiricism* involves the standard affirmation that all knowledge is based on observation or experiment and deals with matters of fact, and that there are no "infallibly known" or "indubitable" propositions or "truths of reason" or the like, but it also takes in much more than this. His complete rejection of philosophical rationalism and its belief in ontological *ultimates* of one kind or another, leads him to criticise various so-called "empiricists" including the "British Empiricists". Thus he rejects all forms of ontological monism, dualism and atomism, main-

[1] For more details see Anderson's *Studies in Empirical Philosophy*. For an interesting statement of his position in a single article compare also J.A.B. Holland, "A System of Classical Atheism", *Scottish Journal of Theology*, August 1973, pp. 271–94.

taining that there is, in this sense, neither the One, the Two, nor the Many, but *none*, that is, there are no ultimates. Whatever exists is on *the same level of reality* as anything else that exists. His *pluralism*, which is also a criticism of rationalism, is a "pluralistic logic of events" that affirms the complexity and plurality of everything that exists. Contrary to monism again, there are real differences between things, contrary to atomism there are real connections between things, and contrary to both there is no ultimate simple, or set of ultimate simples, to which *complex situations* can be reduced. What exists is an infinite number of spatio-temporal situations, that are independently real, but are interrelated, and each of which is a complex network of qualities and relations.

Anderson's theory of the categories is derived largely from Kant, Hegel and Alexander. Samuel Alexander, 1859–1938, who was born in Sydney and left Australia as a young man, strongly influenced Anderson when he gave the Gifford Lectures at Glasgow University in 1916–1917. These lectures were subsequently written up and published in Alexander's *Space, Time and Deity*. The book was not as influential a realist work as it might have been, partly because, as Anderson points out, Alexander made too many concessions to idealism and concentrated too much on exposition and too little on criticising other views and arguing for his own position. Anderson himself sought to repair the deficiencies of Alexander's account by developing a thoroughgoing realistic view of "Space, Time and the Categories", but he never completed his project of writing a book on the subject, and there is little coverage of it in his articles, though he did deal with the subject at length in his lectures.

In broad outline, Alexander's and Anderson's overall position may be described most simply as a reconstruction of Kant's system of philosophy in a realist way. Kant, it may be said, sought to effect a compromise between idealism and realism— though it was a compromise that favoured idealism. Thus, according to him, what we know are "phenomena" which have several ingredients or sources of supply; the "raw material" is supplied by unknowable, outside "things in themselves", but the general forms or conditions of phenomena, namely, space and time, and the categories, are supplied by the human mind (by "intuition" and "understanding" respectively). The idealist, Hegel, tries to overcome certain difficulties in Kant's system by eliminating "things in themselves", so that everything that exists becomes a form of mind or consciousness, but the realists,

Alexander and Anderson, proceed in the opposite way, by eliminating mind-dependent ingredients and affirming that there are only "things in themselves", that is, *things as they are* which are real and knowable. So in Anderson's view,[2] the philosophical theory of space, time and the categories is a theory about the forms or conditions of complex situations or occurrences in general. Along with spatio-temporality, which is the medium in which all things are, the categories—which include identity, difference, particularity, universality, structure, quality, relation, causality, quantity and number—are pervasive or interpenetrating forms or conditions of all that is. Space, time and all the categories apply to *all* situations, whether they are pre-eminently physical, biological, psychological, social, or whatever, but by extension we can also speak of more special categories that apply in a more restricted way, or to more restricted types of situation, for example the particular categories that obtain in physics, biology etc., and, similarly, in social science. Consequently there can be study and criticism of the categories both in the case of the forms of all situations and of the forms of particular types of situations, and it is vital, Anderson argues, for the scientist to have a sense of the categories.

> If the work of inquiry is to be carried on, it must be *at once* scientific and philosophic, . . . if, in particular, the scientist is not philosophic, he will fall into confusions, he will rebuff philosophic criticism—he will lack a theory of categories, of sorts of problem, of "method"—especially he will be carried away by practical interests, by the interest in producing something or implementing a programme instead of in finding something out. (S p. 183)

In the case of social science, then, an awareness of categorial questions must accompany the marshalling of specific truths about social material; and in Anderson's own case his social thought offers a contribution to both of these undertakings. Much of his social theory is concerned with criticising categorial con-

[2] Anderson's view has much in common with Alexander's but he criticises him on the following main counts. (1) Alexander is insufficiently realistic when he agrees with Descartes and the idealists that the mind's knowledge of itself has a different logical status from that of knowledge of other things; (2) in regarding space-time as the "matrix" or "stuff" of things, Alexander is suggesting a monistic "receptacle" or "substance" view of space-time; (3) in his dubious doctrine of "point-instants" he is implying, in an atomistic way, that these are non-complex "pure particulars" or "simples"; (4) his doctrine of emergent qualities, including those he refers to as "Deity", suggests a rationalistic conception of degrees or levels of reality.

fusions and seeking to establish what he takes to be the correct
account of the social categories, but he also offers various specific
theories and explanations, including a number that are derived
by revising Marx's empirical contentions in a pluralist way, and
others that are based on Anderson's observations about the role
of moral factors in society.

What, according to Anderson, are the categories that hold in
the social field? In the first place, there are all the categories
that apply to social situations *qua* their being situations, including,
notably, causality and particularity and universality. Thus in
the social field no less than in the field of any other phenomena
determinism obtains—though, as will emerge, various confusions
about determinism and indeterminism in the social field have to
be cleared up. Likewise, *generality* exists and *regularities* are present
in the social as well as the non-social field. The contrary view
that there is an incompatibility between "uniqueness" and
"recurrence"—or that there can't be regularities because history does not "repeat itself"—involves a thoroughly confused
position. For, in Anderson's view, no occurrence, social or
otherwise, is purely unique or purely simple; any occurrence
is a complex state of affairs which, in *occurring* at all—and not
merely in *recurring*—already has general as well as special characteristics. "There are no separate regions of the universal and
the particular, but any situation exhibits both particularity and
generality."[3] (S p. 172) Thus, individual men, mice, mountains
and motor cars have, in their properties or ways of behaving,
both regularities and peculiarities, continuities and discontin-
uities, and the same is true of social phenomena. Whether we are
dealing, say, with armies, oligarchies, members of parliament,
economic depressions, colonial settlements or religious movements, in each case any particular phenomenon has peculiarities
or special attributes of its own, but at the same time has general
features or ways of working in common with other phenomena of
its type—otherwise, for one thing, it would be inexplicable why
we so often succeed in identifying as "armies", "oligarchies"
and so on, the various historical phenomena that go under these
names. History does repeat itself, not wholesale, but in part,
and that is why we are able to locate definite areas of social
investigation and why there are social or historical regularities
ready for the finding—although these may well be *complex*, not

---

[3] In addition to Anderson's writings on universals, see, for example, T.A. Rose, "The
Nominalist Error", *A.J.P.P.*, August 1949.

simple, contrary to what is so often crudely assumed by historians, and others, when they argue about whether or not there are "laws" in history.

To make these preliminary categorial observations is equivalent to saying that social science has a definite subject matter, but saying that, of course, still leaves open various empirico-social possibilities. Not that there is a hard and fast line here between questions about "general" and "special" categories —confusions about indeterminism and the absence of "laws" in particular, Anderson emphasises, carry over into and constantly clutter up social thought—but we need, in the second place, to concentrate on the problems or preoccupations specific to social science by asking what are its key terms and propositions, and what are the errors and illusions it commonly has to contend with. Anderson's answer to the last question, expressed broadly, is that social science must reject the confused doctrines of (1) "voluntarism"—the view that what happens flows from what is "willed" or voluntarily decided on by human beings; (2) "individualism" or "social atomism"—the view that the human individual is the "unit" or "atom" or basic subject matter of social science; and (3) "solidarism"—the view that society is a single, unitary or harmonious thing. Expressed positively, we must correspondingly affirm social determinism and social pluralism, the latter in the two connected senses (1) of recognising the importance of social institutions, organisations and ways of life, and (2) of recognising the variety of social forces and the importance of the conflicts among them.

It may be helpful to note here a point concerning Anderson's terminology. In his writings he has a penchant for using barely explained technical labels—in general as well as social philosophy. This probably contributes to the difficulty some readers have in understanding him. It is not surprising that his writings often seem unclear considering that he wrote mainly for people already schooled in his views and terminology. His terminology is not, however, idiosyncratic; the position is that the standard "-isms" of orthodox philosophy are often unclear or even incoherent in that they embrace competing views or assumptions. Anderson's procedure, therefore, is to elect what he took to be a defensible view of the "-ism" and to pay little attention to discarded versions of it. This has already been briefly explained in the case of his understanding of "realism", "empiricism" and "pluralism", and the same is true of "determinism" and the various social "-isms" that he refers to. Once this is made clear it is, I believe, rewarding to make full use of Anderson's preferred terminology, not only to provide us with shorthand devices that save long repetitions, but also to keep before us Anderson's feeling for the importance of adopting broad, definite positions. That procedure, too, enables potential critics to locate quickly any major areas of disagreement.

CRITICISMS OF VOLUNTARISM, ATOMISM AND SOLIDARISM

Social Voluntarism

The theory—or, more often, the unexamined assumption—of social voluntarism, Anderson maintains, commonly occurs along with individualism. The two are linked ingredients in the outlook, often exhibited not only by the ordinary unreflective voter in the street, but also by many politicians, editorialists and intellectuals generally, according to which social and political arrangements are the outcome of the voluntary wishes, strivings or decisions of the various separate individuals who compose society. Voluntarism Anderson rejects in general as a form of indeterminism. On the theory of pure voluntarism all would be quite arbitrary and unpredictable, we could never give any explanation of why some given act of willing occurred or some given decision was made; but equally, he argues, on a theory of "impure" or "mixed" voluntarism, that is, one in which uncaused willings were combined with caused events, what happened would still be arbitrary and inexplicable for there would be no way of telling when "uncaused" factors would or would not intervene to influence outcomes. (Compare S pp. 122–25.)

Apart from criticism of the general theory of uncaused "free will", there are the evident difficulties that face the voluntarist conception of *society* according to which social conditions are determined, or indeed constituted, by personal decisions. In criticism of this Anderson refers to "the standard arguments against voluntarism", which are often unknown, even to educated people, who "do not understand that, if social conditions depend on the voluntary decisions which are made from time to time, there can be nothing properly called social or political *theory*, but merely *annals*, records of the various decisions made by various persons at various times—a source from which little in the way of critical thinking can spring". (S pp. 198–99) A well-known example of the social errors of voluntarism, coupled with those of individualism, is found in "Social Contract" theories of the origin of society. The notion that society arose from arrangements deliberately made or contracted into by human beings "implies the pre-existence of society" (S p. 227), and likewise, mention of "'the principles upon which the nation has been founded' suggests that at one time these 'principles' were a subject of discussion, and that a definite conclusion was arrived at . . . But [that] is not so; no general agreement on the political structure of society has ever been come to, and the reference to a supposed underlying agreement is merely a way of avoiding discussion of political fundamentals." (OF p. 11) More complex and more contemporary, but no less erroneous, is the position of the voluntarist social reformer, including past and present utopian or philanthropic Socialists. There is a close, but often unnoticed, parallel here between the reformer's assumptions and the assumptions classically made about the role of the I or ego in making "free choices" between competing lines of activity. The ego in fact is not "free" or perfectly "reasonable", but itself a particular form of activity that is in a strategic position which enables it to put its force on one side rather than another.[4] Likewise, then, the social philanthropist wrongly believes that he is above or outside society and can intervene as he wishes, but in fact he himself is subject to social conditions and what he does involves taking sides and is limited by existing circumstances. That is the kind of criticism advanced by Marx against the "Utopian Socialists" like Robert Owen, for example, in the third of his *Theses on Feuerbach*. The argument there is summed up by Anderson as follows—though with a concluding comment that shows his lack of unqualified admiration for Marx:

> It is impossible to divide society into active and passive sections (whether conceived, implausibly enough, as *helpers and helped* or in any other manner), . . . there is no one who is merely a victim of circumstances and no one who is completely a master of circumstances, . . . there is inter-

[4] Compare a comment by Anderson on Spinoza, *A.J.P.P.*, December 1937, p. 304.

action at all points. Or at least this last is the natural conclusion of the Thesis, but it is somewhat obscured and confused through Marx's obsession with the revolutionary re-making of society and the conflictless Utopia which he expects to see emerging. (S p. 198)

Determinism, then, applies to human beings; all of them are subject to the interplay of social and other forces whether we are considering reformers and other social "interventionists", or the other men who are the recipients of their intervention, or whether, more widely, we are considering men in terms of their transactions with non-human material. The voluntarist suggestion is "that things go on in their historical way until at some point 'we' step in and alter their direction for the better—or the worse", but, Anderson goes on:

> We do not, in fact, step out of the movement of things, ask "What am I to do?" and, having obtained an answer, step in again. All our actions, all our questionings and answerings are part of the movement of things; and if we can work on things, things can work on us—if they can be our "vehicles", we also can be vehicles; social and other forces can work through us. (S p. 241)

This last comment introduces what for Anderson is an important conception of social forces, such as movements and institutions, whose ways of working, he wants to insist, are contrary to voluntarism. It is these social forces, for example, that falsify the utopian assumption that we can, by rational persuasion, get men to change society. Persuasion, Anderson argues, is not "a universal method. Persuasion is possible only between persons with joint activities, participants in a common organisation. It does not work in the case of opposed forms of organisation." (FT p. 3) Moreover, he argues, in a crucial statement of his position:

> A way of life is not something that we adopt, by a voluntary decision, but something that adopts us, takes us as a vehicle, kindles a certain "spirit" in us. Thus the scientific spirit, the spirit of inquiry, may be said to be kindled in us by the scientific movement, by a social phenomenon which no individual or set of individuals could have planned. (S p. 266)

Now in the case of social phenomena of this kind a version of voluntarism is the view that they have been planned or designed to, and in fact fulfil, certain ends or purposes. Anderson repudiates that view and argues that there are various social forces which, while they embrace individuals, have their own definite, un-designed and unpurposeful, ways of working. Criticism of the view can be made on several counts, but a primary point is that many social movements and institutions were manifestly *not* planned or designed. The development of the modern State is an important instance; an acute thinker like Machiavelli may have foreseen (and supported) some features of the States that were to come, but the same insights can hardly be attributed to the actual historical figures involved in various countries. Take, as well-known examples, the development of the State in England in the 1530s and in France in the 1630s and the leading men concerned, Henry VIII and Thomas Cromwell and Louis XIII and Cardinal Richelieu. Even the most able man among them, Richelieu, cannot be said to have clearly grasped what he was doing—consider his religious justifications of his actions—and in any case a variety of people were involved in each country, most of them being quite confused about what they were imple-menting or opposing; so that, all in all, while it emerged that the King's power was increasing at the expense of the feudal nobility, no one could be said to be deliberately constructing the modern State apparatus; what the actions of these people set in motion was the development of an institution with its own complex, unanticipated ways of working. Again, in more recent times, the deliberate creation of States, for example, Israel and some of the new African countries, has been attended by quite unplanned developments and problems. Likewise, for example, the emergence of a strong English Parliament, the growth of the different churches, or the rise of nationalist movements cannot plausibly be claimed to be the outcome of contrivance or design. They may, of course, in part have been initially started off with certain purposes in mind, but these are not what ultimately became characteristic of them. Moreover, even those institutions which were specifically started off, to do certain jobs, such as standing armies, bureaucracies, police forces, trade unions or political parties, have quickly come to have a variety of "pur-poses"—that is, actual social functions—including ones that were unintended and undesired by their founders. The same, for that matter, applies also to more narrowly oriented institutions like those concerned with sport. What is the purpose now of the Olympic Games? If it has one it is also notoriously evident that it has come to be an arena for the assertion of nationalistic and political interests. Likewise with, to pick a more mundane example, the Australian Jockey Club. This may continue with its original purpose of conducting race meetings, but it is clear that it has various functions and there are various interests connected with it, including conflicting and even irreconcilable ones. Even peripheral organisations of this kind, we may argue, falsify voluntarism; they mirror faithfully in microcosm some of the varied and unplanned features of more complicated and more significant social forces.

Social Atomism

At this point issues about voluntarism merge into ones about individualism or social atomism and lead us into a separate consideration and criticism of that subject. Once it becomes evident that social forms or forces like institutions and other organisations are not in vital ways planned or designed, the next step is to recognise that their existing and continuing ways of working are of such a kind that, in important respects, it may be said that they mould or direct the separate individuals who belong to them, rather than that the reverse relation holds.

The term "individualism" is sometimes used to refer to the moral, political or economic *policy* of advocating or defending the "freedom" or "rights" of the individual in relation to the State, authority, or other body. But in his social theory Anderson —in line with Marx's thought—understands by the term a mistaken theory about the social *nature* of men or the part they *actually* play in society and history. Thus, while he himself in his social policies trenchantly defends the political liberty and the freedom of speech and thought of the individual, he also places much stress on the basic importance of institutions, movements, and so on, contrary, for example, to utilitarians like John Stuart Mill or individualist anarchists like Shelley and Stirner who, while they defend the liberty and "rights" of the individual, at the same time assume an essentially individualist view about the nature or structure of society and its ingredient social forces. A philosophical connection of individualism as a social theory that Anderson particularly notes is the one it has with Descartes' doctrine that every man is a self-sufficient, thinking essence. It is no accident, he holds, that the *cogito* became prominent in a period of rising economic individualism, and he further connects the Cartesian legacy with individualism in psychology, that is, the unitary view of man that takes him not "as a complex of interrelated processes" but as having an "'ego' standing above and directing, instead of *being* processes". (RA p. 161) Individualism, moreover, in both popular and learned social and political thought, has had, and still has, an influence that can scarcely be exaggerated, and with it go various assumptions about social practice and social intervention that Anderson seeks to expose as illusory. Accordingly, it is imperative for the progress of social science to pin down and criticise this exceedingly widespread view.

This view, *social individualism*, or more unambiguously, *social atomism*, is the view that there are really no social forces except persons. What pass as other "social forces" are social resultants, not determinants, that is, society as a whole, and lesser ingredients of society like institutions, organisations, classes and movements, are all aggregates of fundamentally unitary individuals. Now this view is confronted by many difficulties, an initial one being that of accounting for the origin of communities. It has to adopt the "untenable theory of the establishment of community by the coming together of originally separate individuals" (S p. 348), whether we have an individualism of the "Social Contract" kind or a less simple view. An example of the latter is Sigmund Freud's claims about the dominant place of violence in founding and maintaining society, to which Anderson retorts that the sociality of man is there to begin with, that while there may be many violent individuals, "even in the smallest community, brute force cannot be the decisive factor—unless there is 'moral force', unless there are established ways of working, there is not a community" and again, as Engels argues, "'the coming of weapons' implies a type of social organisation capable of producing them". (S p. 349) All the more surely, then, in advanced society the inescapable sociality of man makes him not simply an active individual agent but also to a very considerable degree "a 'vehicle' of social forces, . . . a member of movements which are just as real, just as definite as he is". (S p. 341) Anderson cites with approval (S p. 342) Nietzsche's statement: "It is very obvious that the ultimate and smallest 'individuals' cannot be understood in the sense of metaphysical atoms; their sphere of power is continually shifting its ground." Further, as against the atomistic observation that "the individuals who make up society do not get fused or transmuted, as in chemical combination",[5]

[5] Made by H.B. Acton, *The Illusion of the Epoch*, London, Cohen and West, 1955, p. 155.

Anderson argues in a key formulation, "the answer is that forms of activity do get fused and transmuted, and so far from there being social atoms who can merely form a 'mechanical mixture', it is such forms of activity that make up 'individuals'". (RA p. 162) Likewise, when we study man's conflicting and divisive activities which, along with his co-operative and communicative activities are part and parcel of social life, we find their true locus to be these real and definite forms of social activity:

> Social struggle . . . consists in the opposition not of individuals but of forms of organisation (which, of course, develop in the course of struggle, as working-class organisations have conspicuously done). It is above all as members of such organisations or institutions that individuals develop their activities and hence formulate demands; it is not from individual demands that institutions arise. No doubt there are some institutions, such as the family, which do more than others to foster an individualistic outlook; but at any rate, forms of association are the primary social fact. (SS p. 4)

So, contrary to social atomism, the subject matter of social science is not individuals conceived as "units" or "atoms". The true subject is forms of social activity; "social science is precisely the account of their interrelations, their changes, their continuance or cessation, and, incidentally, of their effects, but there is no point in calling these effects their 'purposes'." (S p. 344)

There are certain variants of the individualist approach, such as "the great man theory" or "the conspiracy theory" of history, about which Anderson did not say a great deal, but criticisms of which are implicit in his position. In this kind of view it is assumed less that individual persons in the mass, or even large numbers of them, are socially or historically influential, but that it is the leader, or else an elite group of men—for example leading members of an oligarchy or a governing class—that largely engineer or manipulate social developments. Such a view, of course, ignores the role social forces have in shaping and limiting the activities of individual men, including those of the most powerful leaders, and once more entails the voluntarist belief that certain men are outside history or exempt from social conditions. Leaders, Anderson maintains, do influence the course of historical events in definite ways—for, as will emerge in discussing his pluralist view of social determinism, he disagrees with Marxists like Engels who seek to play down altogether the role of historical leadership. Nevertheless, in his view, leaders are not cut off from the people they lead; their initiation and sponsorship of policies and the like occurs within parties, movements and organisations; in other words, leadership, although it is in the hands of strategically placed and sometimes able individual men, is an objective social phenomenon that is subject to and limited by the interplay of social forces and conditions.

Social atomism and voluntarism, it may be observed in summing up, are interwoven conceptions of society, but are still different or separable views. It is hard to find an expression of social voluntarism that is not also a version of individualism; perhaps the "theological" view of history, or, again, Hegel's doctrine of "The Cunning of Reason" will serve; that is, the contention that what happens in history is freely willed or intended by something other than men, namely by God or Absolute Reason—though it might be contended instead that these are really personified entities and hence that we merely have variants of the "great man" theory of history. However, individualism without voluntarism is easier to find, for example, within Freudian theory. Thus most Freudian writers adopt—or claim to adopt—a determinist view according to which men's decisions, wishes, and so on, are entirely determined by mental and other causes, but at the same time, if they do come to advance a social theory they normally do so in highly individualistic (as distinct from organisational etc.) terms. But in any case the two views, voluntarism and individualism, are different in content; the one attaches great importance to "free" or "unconditioned" *decisions*, the other to the assumption that separate *individuals* are the only real social forces; the two come together, as Anderson stresses, in much of what passes for "social theory".

Solidarism

"Solidarism",[6] Anderson maintains, is another prominent unscientific assumption often held in conjunction with individualism and voluntarism, but different from them. For example, "whereas voluntarism would make the facts amenable to any sort of

[6] The term "solidarisme" appears to have been coined and popularised early this century by the French educationalist, F. Buisson. He, following H. Marion's doctrine of "moral solidarity", meant by "solidarism" what he regarded as the basic "harmony" between the classes or between the individual and society. See, for example, F. Buisson, *Un Moraliste Laïque, Pages Choisies*, Paris, 1933, p. 163.

arrangement, solidarism proposes an 'ideal' (the reconciliation of all interests) above the facts and dictating their arrangements 'for the best'". (SS p. 4) According to it, "society is constituted by all ... standing together for mutual aid"; "it assumes the solid society which can bring about 'desirable' ends". (TW pp. 3–4) As such it is a "'monistic' point of view" which contrasts with "the 'pluralistic' point of view in which society is regarded as a multiplicity of interrelated groups".[7] (TW p. 5)

Solidarism must be distinguished from the *solidarity* that a particular group or class may exhibit—as when it carries on co-operative, productive, or "heroic" activities. That is, while Anderson stresses the role of struggle and tension in society (as against the "harmonious", or "philanthropic" assumptions made by the solidarist or social monist), he does of course recognise the existence, and the equal importance within certain areas of society, of co-operation or solidarity. But just as there is no single activity, or no single set of activities, which is the work or business of society, there is no such thing as an overall solidarity, or social unity, or total interest, that applies to the whole of society. The view that Anderson here rejects—and rejecting it is a vital part of his social theory—has commonly been ventilated in past and present society in connection with claims or assumptions made about the primacy in society of "common interests", including an "imaginary 'common good' (something that satisfies every interest and every person)". (S p. 191) In the solidarist view, society as such has a general interest or good, or a set of common interests or goods which, in more grandiose metaphysical formulations, has been described as an overriding "purpose" or "aim" designed or pursued, for example by God or Absolute Spirit, or more mundanely but still metaphysically as being found in the "general will" or in "the greatest good of the greatest number". This last, utilitarian conception is the one that has had a widespread influence on modern political thought, and it is this that Anderson criticises in an article he devoted to Bentham.

According to Bentham, utility is supposed to be the principle which will enable us to decide what are to be the objects of

---

[7] This quotation is taken from an essay sympathetic to Communism in which Anderson sought to contrast the theory of the revolutionary working class with both solidarism and pluralism. However, my concern here is to expound Anderson's mature thought (his early Communist views are dealt with in Part II), and his remarks in the essay in question anticipate his later unqualified pluralism, when he regarded Communism itself as a form of solidarism or social monism.

approbation or pursuit, but, Anderson argues, Bentham's account of "pleasure" is not clear or definite and his principle does not provide "a common measure" in the required way.

> Certainly, [he writes] there can be an adjustment between different demands of a particular person, just as there can be between demands of different persons. But we cannot bring all demands to a single "market", and, in order to see what demands will be effective, we have to take account of the whole interplay of social forces; and as far as "quantity of pleasure" is concerned, measurement can be made only after the event. To estimate the keenness of a demand we have to see how far people are prepared to go to get it satisfied; we have to let competing demands *fight it out*. (S p. 229)

There is, then, no "single market" for demands, or no actual general interest that overrides particular interests, though the *claim* that there is may have a substantial socio-political role. Thus, an appeal to "our" or "everyone's interest" may mislead people into supporting particular interests, opposed to their own particular interests, because they become convinced that the former are general or common interests; and this is a consideration of vital importance in politics. Contrary to Bentham, the legislator's function "cannot be conceived as that of a universal calculator or seeker of 'general welfare'". There is no one "whose interest is the general interest" and "the legislator is simply a person who has certain demands of his own and certain special ways of getting them satisfied; in particular, that of annexing 'pains' or penalties to any opposition to his demands". (S p. 231) There is, therefore, a parallel between what Anderson says here about the legislator and what he says elsewhere about the utopian reformer, and, as with the latter, misconceptions about the legislator's actual role can have definite political effects: "It may quite well be in the legislator's interest, that is, it may advance his schemes, to put about the notion of public welfare and the supposition that he is acting with that object in view; he may even put it in that way to himself, but it is not so." (S p. 231) As specific examples, Anderson argues, when Bentham upholds the essential goodness of public *order* and private *property*, it is not difficult to show what *special* interests —as against the interests of all—are the ones being defended.

To recapitulate these points in a wider context, the anti-solidarist position is that there is no general interest or common good in the required sense of being that of society itself, and recurrently fashionable appeals to this interest or good in an attempt to settle public issues, while they may be *politically* effective, are *logically* deficient in two connected ways. One arises from the tautological nature of the appeals made. Owing to the "democratic" or "egalitarian" nature of the appeals it is normally assumed that people generally are in a position to recognise or understand the general interests involved. However, in that case, if supporting (or opposing) interest or measure X is really in the general interest or the interest of us all, then to ask us to support X is to ask us to support what we already support. But, of course, appeals to "the welfare of the community", "the interests of all Australians" and so on, are notoriously made precisely when there is a patent conflict between the advancement of interest X and the advancement of some other interest Y, and an effort is being made to induce supporters of Y to change and support X. (Compare everyday controversies about drinking, drugs, divorce, abortion, and the like.) Second, the efficacy of these efforts largely depends on a clouding of the issues by making it appear that there really is an overriding general interest at stake (as when, in popular controversies, some people are made to feel confused, or that they are in some way wrong or unnatural because they are inclined to oppose "the best interests of the nation" etc.). In his earlier writings Anderson took a substantially Marxist view of the social interests furthered by this kind of deception or obfuscation, maintaining for example that "all activities or proposals of a solidarist character, all schemes of 'class-collaboration' or social unity, are for the benefit of the ruling class and for the deception of the workers". (TW p. 6) But as he came to question the simple Marxist theory of economic classes and to widen his pluralism by emphasising organisations, movements and ways of life, he correspondingly recognised that it is not only capitalist interests, but a *variety* of special interests, including supposedly "radical" and "humanitarian" ones, that can be given strength when they masquerade as "the general interest".

If, the solidarist—or "monistic" or "totalistic"—view of social life is not true, and society is not a single, solid or unitary thing possessing some overall, general or total aim or interest, are there not nevertheless certain "general interests" that can be identified, such as the provision of ordinary "communal needs" by the State? Anderson's answer is that while we can, in a fashion, speak in this way of the general or common interest, what is meant by it must be scrutinised carefully. As is well known to critics of traditional political philosophy, discussions not only about "natural rights" or about "the sovereign will of the people", but even of such obvious apparent "interests of us all" as fresh air or good health, lead us straight back to an inevitable pluralism of special interests. Consider how contemporary disputes about air and water pollution, or about national health schemes, plainly reveal the existence of conflicts between irreconcilable actual interests and of conflicts between irreconcilable views about preferred ways of living. (Compare, in the case of health, questions about government funding of medical costs vis-à-vis other projects, the interests of patients, doctors, nurses, and, for example of those who create industrial pollutants, or, again, the kind of issue raised by Bernard Shaw when he said "It's not how long you live but *how* you live" that matters.) In these circumstances, appeal to the supposed general interest, as noted above, merely masks the promotion of certain interests or alignments of forces at the expense of others. Any reference to the "general interest" is thus likely to have built into it a continuing, question-begging suggestion of its primacy or superiority. However, suppose we do understand that interest in a definite, empirical way as referring to the provision of health, security and public necessities for the population as a whole, then, Anderson argues, it by no means follows that this kind of interest is an overriding or fundamental one. Furthering the needs of the whole community—which all too often also means implementing the most consumptive and unthinking aspirations of the majority of the population—involves the furtherance of a certain kind of "communal" interest or way of living that is not as high as certain other special interests or ways of living. "The level of the general interest", Anderson insists, "is one of mediocrity and, where that interest is allowed to absorb special interests, mediocrity spreads" and " 'community service', high-sounding though it may be, is a *low* ideal". (PD pp. 8–9) A longer passage sums up his position and brings out his objection to the reductionist contentions of solidarism:

> Some will argue, in this connection, that the common interest comes first, that, unless the State is secure, special interests cannot be satisfied, that they are merely the *trimmings* of public life—a point which, it would be suggested, is forcibly brought home to us in a time of emergency. This is similar to the view of certain Marxists that the necessities of life must be secured before there can be any

question of culture. Now these contentions cannot be accepted unconditionally; liberty and culture are quite frequently upheld at the expense of security and "common necessities", and unless people were prepared to take this line, there would be no liberty or culture worth speaking of. It is true that unless we live, we cannot live well, but false that we must devote ourselves first to living and afterwards to living well. And even what are generally recognised as necessities are not on that account the most important things in life; on the contrary, their place in life is that of *means*, of things subsidiary to people's main interests. (PD pp. 8–9)

ETHICS

Criticisms of Traditional Ethics

The quotation at the end of the last chapter reveals the connection Anderson's pluralism has with his theory of ethics—it is not merely that there are many diverse and competing social activities and interests, there is the further fact that some of them are, and some of them are not, intrinsically *good*.

Normally the studies of ethics and social theory have little to do with one another. As Anderson points out, the first notable ethical theorist, Socrates, was disadvantaged by his lack of awareness of social issues, while his opponents, the Greek Sophists, although for their part weak on ethics, did draw attention in a way Socrates did not to the highly significant part played by social factors in shaping human beliefs. The antithesis between these two kinds of outlook has persisted since then, more or less undiminished. As any perusal of the history of moral philosophy amply confirms, ethical theorists have little acquaintance with serious social theory, and conversely, the few able social theorists that history has thrown up have displayed little interest in, or indeed have been contemptuous of, the positive study of ethics. In the case of traditional moral philosophers, of course, their sheering away from social theory was a natural outcome of their preoccupation with laying down certain precepts or norms, for if they had paid attention to even elementary social findings —for example, those of Machiavelli or Marx—they could scarcely have failed to notice the concealed social and political content of their own moral pronouncements. But it is not only the traditionalists who have been at fault. The same absence of an aware social theory is a conspicuous feature of "up to date" contemporary moral philosophers, including not least the "linguistic" ones, and is a consequence, Anderson argues, of their mostly unexamined assumption of the truth of social atomism, voluntarism and solidarism. With Anderson himself, however, we have the rare case of a thinker with a vital interest in both ethics and social science—indeed, only Georges Sorel among noteworthy social theorists had something of a comparable combination of interests, but he was not, strictly speaking, an ethical theorist or analyst. Thus, Anderson's analysis and criticism of traditional ethics was not accompanied by a rejection of the subject itself as one—like theology in the atheist's view—whose primary preoccupations are instances of ideology or illusion; he does hold that almost all past ethical thought is guilty, overtly or covertly, of "the fraud of moralism", but there nevertheless exists a positive science of ethics, and this science has close affiliations with social science: (1) because in a general way they are both naturalistic studies of related social phenomena; and (2) because of the particular connection there is between the identification of certain human activities as qualitatively good and the study of the characteristics of social movements and ways of life.

Just as there are barriers to social science that have first to be removed, so too with ethics. Relativist confusions have to be cleared away to make possible the development of ethical science. As mentioned earlier, "relativism" is a term used by Anderson to describe an important type of confusion about qualities and relations, and in the case of ethics the key relativist error lies in confusing or amalgamating the qualitative question, Is X good? with relational questions about X's being wanted, or supported, or being brought about by human beings. In seeking to reject relativism and replace it by an objective science of ethics, he is at variance with the *normative* or *prescriptive* approach to ethics that has dominated the entire history of moral philosophy. In the normative view, the job of ethics is to tell us *what we ought to do* and it characteristically tries to do so by setting up "norms" or "ideals" which are justified by some ultimate authority or principle such as God, Obligation, the Moral End, the Categorical Imperative or Moral Intuition.

Now, as Anderson brings out, this normative position is vulnerable to a number of criticisms which I will classify as two subordinate criticisms and a third, more fundamental one. First, there is the question of the metaphysical assumptions about God, Obligation and so on, made by the leading moral theories. "They all assume certain higher moral powers *whereby* historical events can have moral characteristics in a secondary sense, just as the metaphysician assumes an ultimate reality whereby historical appearances can have a subordinate reality and be graciously permitted to appear." (S p. 240) Here the objection, in line with empiricist criticism of rationalistic views about levels of reality, is that these supposed ultimates whether metaphysical or moral do not in fact exist. As there is only one way or level of being, that of *occurrence*, "all the objects of science, including minds and goods, are things occurring in space and time" and "all ideals, ultimates, symbols, agencies and the like are to be rejected, and no such distinction as that of facts and principles, or facts and values, can be maintained". (S p. 14)

Second, the supposed relevance of the moralist's moral pronouncements to human conduct is falsified by the actual facts of the "moral life". The voluntarist assumptions he makes about the control people have over their conduct leads the moralist to postulate a special realm of Freedom which leaves moral choices exempt from the laws of causality. Such a position, as already noted, Anderson rejects as indefensible, because, *inter alia*, the constant possibility of arbitrary intervention in the human field by this supposed uncaused factor would preclude the scientific study not only of ethical phenomena but of social affairs generally. Good, Anderson argues, is a social force subject to conditions like other social forces, and "What is done, whether it is good or not, will be determined by the forces that exist." (S p. 242) The moralist is, moreover, mistaken in his assessment of the place in human life of such things as "moral deliberation" and "moral exhortation"; the extent of their occurrence and influence is considerably less than he imagines; but in any case they are subject to causality in the same way as other occurrences. For example, "deliberation arises from a certain opposition of motives. And these opposed motives, in struggling to find outlet, excite other motives which assist them, until one set overcomes the other and acts. Or, again, certain parts of the opposed motives may find common outlet, while other parts are repressed. In either case we have the opposition of two complex tendencies, and a final movement arising from some solution of the opposition." (S p. 220) Again, despite the authoritarian moralist, "The spontaneous action of a motive in seeking its objective cannot be induced by compulsion. Compulsion can only induce conformity. And the motives which will incline a man to conform, to do a thing because he is obliged, are, generally speaking, fear and that desire for self-abasement which, in sexual theory, is called 'masochism'." (S p. 225) Nor, despite the assumptions made by moral solidarists from Socrates onwards, is there any guarantee of the triumph of *good*. "Goodness is *supported* by those good activities already in existence, which encourage the development of other good activities. But in so doing they meet with obstructions, and there is nothing in the nature of things to show that good will overcome evil." (S p. 226)

Anderson's third and crucial objection to traditional ethics is that its attempted moral justifications are founded on illogicalities. Consider such central justificatory conceptions as "obligation" and "end". The obligatory is taken to be that which is essentially demanded of us and the end as that whose nature it is to be pursued. But these are *relativist* conceptions that promise philosophical content but have none, though they may have hidden social content:

> If the obligatory (whether it is a question of "religious duty" or any other) is *what we are to obey* and the end is *what we are to pursue*, then nothing at all has been said as to what these things themselves are; we do not know what to obey or follow. If, on the other hand, we are not fobbed off with relativist conceptions but are given some specific commands or objectives, then we find them to be just as definite historical events as the things they are related to. In a word, when relativism is removed, we are left with simple historical relations of commanding and seeking—A wants X; B is commanded by C to do Y—and what is moral or good about X or Y does not appear. (S p. 240)

Arguments from "the Moral Law" or similar principles set up by moral philosophers like Socrates and Kant are uniformly fallacious; there is no valid inference from them to the conclusion that certain forms of behaviour are obligatory or virtuous, though the brandishing of such principles encourages confused thinking and makes possible the advancement of certain unspecified social demands; and this is something the ethical inquirer will expose by social criticism; he will say: "This action is not required by 'the good' or by the 'moral law', because there is no such thing; by whom is it demanded, then, and what is his policy?" "It is not surprising", Anderson adds in illustration, "that the Athenians looked for Socrates's political affiliations when he claimed to take the pure moral stand." (S p. 241)

But it was actually Socrates, as Anderson notes, who in one of his other pieces of philosophising points the way for a clearing up of the relativist confusions that have bedevilled the history of ethics. In Plato's *Euthyphro*, Socrates, in the course of an examination of a definition of holiness as what is loved by all the gods, asks whether (1) holiness is loved by the gods because it is holy, or (2) it is holy because it is loved by the gods, and goes on to show that we must opt for (1) if we are to take holiness as a definite type of thing with an intrinsic character of its own —for, according to (2), holiness is something derivative that resides merely in the *attitude* the gods have towards it. In a corresponding way in the case of ethics, then, given that there is such a thing as goodness, we must not confuse the attitudes people may have towards it with a description of what it is itself. As Anderson points out, "It is just through this sort of confusion between our attitudes to things and their own characters, that it has been supposed that ethics has to do with ends. It is possible for us to pursue something which is good, but this could not be significantly said if goodness meant being pursued, or even worthy to be pursued by us." (S p. 217) In the realist terminology of "qualities" and "relations", goodness may stand in various relations to various people (it may be loved, pursued, demanded, commanded, prescribed, opposed, and so on by them) but if, as most moral philosophers have supposed—and Anderson concurs with them in this—goodness is an intrinsic *quality* of things it cannot be defined or explained by reference to the *relations* it has to other things; to try so to define or explain it is to make the fundamental relativist error of confusing or amalgamating qualities with relations.

This relativism is, therefore, not the same as what is usually called "ethical relativism". The latter, Anderson holds, is ordinarily a confused position, but *if* it can be coherently presented it will be what he calls the relational position on good, though he maintains there are formidable difficulties in the way of giving a precise account of the socio-psychological relations assumed by that position. He is also critical of what is called "ethical subjectivism". In his view it is ordinarily a crude version of "ethical relativism" and if it could be sustained it would be once more as a relational view and thus, incidentally, a type of *objective* view, for if the assertion "X is good" could be analysed without residue into relational propositions of the type "Social group A has relation R to way of behaving X" that would be to advance an objective relational view.

Positive Ethics

It is Anderson's object, in exposing relativist confusions, to make the way clear for the positive, qualitative study of ethics. Just as it is plainly one thing to ask what sorts of things are trees or triangles or coloured green and a quite different thing to ask how we can bring about trees or triangles or green things, or whether we want to do so, so it is in the case of goods. What things are good and what are their specific characteristics? These questions form the true subject matter of ethical science, and it is an entirely separate and subsequent question to ask how goods are or can be brought about.

The conflation of these two kinds of question has dominated the entire history of ethics, but it is part of Anderson's position that, in the work of many moral philosophers there has been, albeit in a submerged, unclear way, some recognition of goodness as a quality. Moreover, in some cases this recognition has received explicit mention in their writings, beginning, as mentioned above, with Socrates, who while he advanced an authoritarian and metaphysical view of The Form of the Good and believed, solidaristically, that it must in the end prevail, did introduce the logical distinctions referred to in the *Euthyphro*. Also, Anderson argues, in his view of the *co-operation* between the activities that are good, Socrates had some sense of the positive character of goodness. We can add too that some medieval philosophers, though working in an entirely theological context, kept alive the conception of goodness as an independent quality that cannot be accounted for just by saying, for example, that it is created and commanded by God. But if, then, the conception of good as a quality along with conceptions of what specific things are good, has been kept alive in the ethical tradition, still it has to be judged that Anderson has only two clear predecessors: Cudworth and, especially, G.E. Moore.

Cudworth, the seventeenth century Cambridge Platonist, though assuming the existence of God and the usual Christian account of divine attributes, maintains that the moral characteristics of human activities, even though they are created and willed by God, are what they are, not because of the *arbitrary* command or will of God, but by *nature*. Anderson brings out the force of Cudworth's position in a comment which is also a succinct, brief statement of the case against relativism:

Now if the "arbitrary" view (the doctrine of imposition by

command) is taken, what at most we can admit is being
compelled by a being stronger than us to behave in certain
ways, but there would be no reason for calling these ways
of behaving *good*. If, however, we *have* reason for calling
them good—if we find that to be one of their characters
—then we can develop an ethical theory irrespective of the
commands of God, and the additional information, if we
possessed it, that what is good is demanded of us by God,
would be of no assistance in our study of good things themselves. In fact, however, Churchmen ignore Cudworth's
distinction and *amalgamate* the two notions of "being good"
and "being required of us by God".[8]

Cudworth, furthermore, takes an anti-prescriptive stand in the
contrast he draws between virtue and duty when he says, for
instance: "Love would make the obedience more lasting and more
willing to become the natural disposition and temper of the mind:
this is freedom and liberty; the other is the tiresome task and
slavish imposition of religion."[9] At the same time, although
Cudworth is committed to a Christian version of ethics, his
account of the good life as embracing spontaneity or freedom,
rationality, disinterestedness, orderliness and creativity,[10] has
some affinity with the accounts given by Moore and Anderson.

It was not, however, until the time of G.E. Moore that a
really sharp, conscious break was made with traditional prescriptive ethics. Moore, along with Bertrand Russell, was a
leading figure in the reaction early in this century against
dominant, metaphysical trends in various areas of philosophy
and in his *Principia Ethica*, 1903, wrote a closely argued treatise
criticising his ethical predecessors, particularly utilitarians and
hedonists, and arguing for a new approach to ethics. "I have
tried in this book", Moore points out in his Preface, "to distinguish
clearly two kinds of question, which moral philosophers have
always professed to answer but which, as I have tried to show,
they have almost always confused both with one another and
with other questions." The questions are: (1) What "ought to
exist for its own sake, is good in itself or has intrinsic value"?
and (2) "What kind of actions ought we to perform"? He concentrates in the book on a philosophical analysis of what it is
to have an ethics that is scientific, but does in his last chapter

---

[8] "Religion and the University", *The Australian Highway*, November 1961, p. 53.
[9] Quoted by J.A. Passmore, *Ralph Cudworth*, Cambridge University Press, 1951, p. 68.
[10] Compare Passmore, op. cit., Chapter VI.

present, as he says, "some conclusions, with regard to the proper answer of the question 'What is good in itself?' which are very different from any which have commonly been advocated by philosophers".[11] These conclusions are, in brief, that "personal affection and the appreciation of what is beautiful in Art and Nature are good in themselves",[12] and that "knowledge, though having little or no value in itself, is an absolutely essential constituent in the highest goods, and contributes immensely to their value".[13] It was doubtless because of his emphasis on such secular goods as personal affection and aesthetic enjoyment that Moore's ethics was hailed with enthusiasm by the members of the Bloomsbury Group, Lytton Strachey, Maynard Keynes, Virginia Woolf, and others—for example, Strachey's comment when Moore's book appeared: "I expected when I read it to see posters in the streets announcing the Death of Herbert Spencer and the Fall of Kant. But there was only something about the Duke of Devonshire."[14]

Now Anderson acknowledges the work of Moore in seeking to establish a realistic science of ethics. "The first important attempt to develop such a science", he writes, "was made by Moore in his *Principia Ethica*. Moore endeavoured to found an objective theory of goodness." (S p. 244) Anderson's own examples of goodness (which will be referred to more fully presently) are somewhat similar to Moore's, including love and appreciation, but he agrees with Socrates rather than Moore in making knowledge a key example of a good activity. Nevertheless, Anderson also notes various weaknesses in *Principia Ethica* which stem mainly from the considerable concessions Moore still makes to moralistic ethics. "It has to be acknowledged, however, that there is a great deal of relativism in Moore's theory." (S p. 244) Thus Moore "when he speaks of certain actions as our duty" fails to avoid "the relativism of 'the commanded'" (S p. 242); in his "theory of 'good-as-means'" he mistakenly assumes that "the goodness of a thing brought about confers some sort of value on the bringing of it about";[15] and "Moore in upholding the absolutely desirable or the notion of 'good as an end', is running together relational and non-relational notions". (S pp. 256–57) Then, connected with all of this there is an integral part of

[11] *Principia Ethica*, Cambridge University Press, 1903, pp. vii–ix.
[12] *Principia Ethica*, p. 188.
[13] Op. cit., p. 199.
[14] Quoted by Michael Holroyd, *Lytton Strachey*, London, Heinemann, 1967–68, p. 206.
[15] "Theory and Practice of Morals", *A.J.P.P.*, December 1929, p. 297.

Moore's philosophical position that Anderson wishes entirely to repudiate, which is "his doctrine that good is an indefinable and non-natural object" and his conception of good "as having higher reality than other things". (S p. 244)

This last doctrine is the part of Moore's position that is most often discussed by ethical commentators and reference to it here will, by way of contrast, help to clarify Anderson's position. Moore, although having an empiricist bent in much of his philosophy, subscribed—like Russell and Wittgenstein in their logical atomist days—to a rationalistic belief in the existence of simple notions by means of which complex things can be explained. Thus, in his view, while some things such as a horse, are complex and capable of definition (or analysis), others, like yellow and good "are not complex: they are notions of that simple kind out of which definitions are composed and with which the power of further definition ceases".[16] Good, then, is simple and indefinable but (unlike yellow) it is not a *natural* property so that it is a mistake to define good in terms of any natural object (such as pleasure) and to do so is to fall into the "naturalistic fallacy". But for a man with a reputation for penetrating philosophical analysis Moore is here notoriously unclear—and generations of moral commentators on this part of his work have often not helped to make it clearer. Part of the trouble lies in a certain "over-determination" associated with Moore's application of the label "naturalistic fallacy" to offending views. Thus, he sometimes takes it merely to be "the fallacy which consists in identifying the simple notion which we mean by 'good' with some other notion"[17]—that is, since good is simple and indefinable the fallacy lies in trying to define it as anything, natural *or* non-natural; but then the *naturalistic* part of the fallacy is further supposed to arise from trying to define good, which (according to Moore) is non-natural in terms of something natural. There is also the problem of what exactly Moore means by "natural", as he offers only two brief explanations, one being that the natural is that which can exist *"by itself* in time"[18] (so that the non-natural is something timeless and metaphysical), and the other that the natural is that which "we can touch and see and feel"[19] (so that what is observable, but not by sense-perception in a narrow sense, also becomes "non-natural").

[16] *Principia Ethica*, p. 8.
[17] Op. cit., p. 58.
[18] *Principia Ethica*, p. 41.
[19] Op. cit., p. 110.

Now, Anderson wants to reject *in toto* this part of Moore's thinking as a survival of the rationalistic belief in ultimate simples to which true empiricism is utterly opposed. Without trying to present Anderson's arguments on this subject in detail, I shall confine myself to saying that, starting, for example, with Plato's classic criticisms in the *Theaetetus* of the theory that complexes can be explained by or analysed into simple elements, Anderson argues that all like theories are logically untenable whether found, for example, in Descartes' overt rationalism, Russell's and Wittgenstein's theories of logical atomism or Moore's belief in simples. There are no "absolute simples" or "logical atoms" to which complex situations can be "reduced" and no "ultimate explanations" which explain other things but cannot themselves be explained; on the contrary, whatever exists is complex, observable and capable of being discussed and also of being *defined*. There is no question of *having* to define all the "terms" or "sorts of things" (Anderson often uses these expressions interchangeably) that we have dealings with—as there are no "ultimate" terms any such demand that we give non-circular definitions of all terms leads to a vicious infinite regress. Nevertheless, all terms or sorts of things, including *social* ones, are open to investigation and possible definition—that is, of the complex by the complex. Furthermore, the natural is open to *observation* without this having to be restricted to sense-perception in a narrow sense; we cannot straightforwardly see or smell, etc., the State, trade unions or universities, for instance, but nevertheless social phenomena like organisations and movements and the activities that go on in them, including good activities, are definitely existing, observable, *natural* phenomena. Correspondingly, with reference to what Moore calls our "intuition" of good, this simply amounts to "observation, the direct acquisition of positive knowledge, allowing, of course, that people are as apt to make mistakes about moral facts as about physical facts in general".[20] (S p. 217) On the other side, Moore's account of good as "non-natural", his belief that good, while it "is a property of certain natural objects" itself "is not a natural property",[21] flows from a mistaken belief that good (as Socrates supposed about his "eternal Forms") is a "pure predicate" or "pure

---

[20] Anderson thus rejects, in general, any conception of *infallible* intuition, observation, etc. In his view any observation may possibly be a form of mis-observation owing to the fact that the relation of observing/mis-observing is a relation between two complex phenomena —mind and what it is observing.

[21] *Principia Ethica*, p. 41.

universal" detached in its way of being from natural or ordinary existing things. Probably, Anderson acutely conjectures, it is because Moore, too, is a moralist that he is unwilling to define ethical terms. "The point would seem to be," he writes, "that, if we give an 'ethical' definition of any ethical term, we have what is really no more than an identity ('the worth while is worth while', say), whereas if we give a 'non-ethical' definition of it (if we define it as a 'natural object'), we seem to be destroying ethics; hence moralists like Socrates (and Moore) are unwilling to define such terms." (S p. 260)

This, then, is Anderson's view of what it is to have a science of ethics. The next question is, What are his views on specific ethical matters, in particular, What things have the natural quality good? The answer is that there are certain definite human activities that are of a productive or enterprising character which communicate themselves and co-operate with one another. These are the activities which manifest *productive* or *ethical goods* as distinct from "economic goods" or "goods of consumption", which is a contrast, he points out, reflected in past ethics by the distinction commonly made between disinterestedness and interestedness and more recently by Sorel's distinction between "the ethic of the producer" and "the ethic of the consumer". Specific examples of ethical goods are investigation, aesthetic creation and appreciation, enterprise, liberty, courage and love. In an important formulation of his position Anderson writes:

> The conception of the productiveness of goods leads to the view that production is itself a good; it fulfils the conditions mentioned in the case of investigation, and it also assists and is assisted by investigation. Indeed, we find investigation flourishing where production is developing, and the assistance given by science to production is equally well marked. Similar considerations apply to aesthetic creation and appreciation; in fact the distinction between these forms of activity is hard to draw; the artist and the investigator are producers of a sort, the producer is in some measure an artist and an investigator. But as we broadly distinguish between Science, Art and Industry within a social culture, so we may broadly distinguish scientific, artistic and productive activity. (S p. 245)

Goods, whether we refer to them in a more social way as exhibiting themselves in movements and ways of life or in a more psychological way as forms of mental activities or processes, are marked not by a forced, mechanical or compulsive character, but by enterprise or initiative and by spontaneity or freedom (in a non-metaphysical sense). Liberty, which is a form of goodness, he sums up in one place in this way: "Liberty, then, is the ability to take things artistically, to pursue them for their own sake. It cannot be supported except by itself; there is no other motive to it than these free activities already in existence, in others and in a man's own self. It demands publicity and is opposed to all obscuring and confusing of issues." (EP p. 27) Likewise love, which normally manifests itself in a more psychological or personal than a widely social way, is an essential communicant with all goods. "Feuerbach", Anderson writes in one interesting formulation, "treats love (natural love) as the core of humanity, the central good; and it may be argued, along these lines, that freedom in love is the condition of other freedoms, that while in itself it does not constitute culture, there can be no culture without it, that it continually enriches and is enriched by the various forms of productive (enterprising) activity—Science, Art, Industry." (AM p. 262) These various goods, moreover, are *natural* occurrences, along with the activities or forces opposed to them. Whether goods flourish in particular persons or in societies at large depends, not on the prescriptions of moralists (which are in any case mostly inimical to goodness), but on the interplay of various historical forces; nor, contrary to many moral philosophers, is goodness to be found particularly among those who study or think about ethical theory. "People in general," Anderson points out, "do not think very much about the goodness of their activities. They are simply to be found trying to make discoveries or to produce works of art, exhibiting love or courage, or, on the other hand, imposing obligations on themselves or others, because they are made that way, that is, because their character, in relation to their history, has so developed." (S p. 226)

There is one final question that must be considered, albeit briefly. If the history of moral philosophy, not to speak of religion, is saturated with relativism in its theories and with authoritarianism in its recommendations on conduct, and if, further, there are these human activities that have the specific characteristics Anderson identifies, what is his justification for describing them as *good*—why not, in view of all the errors and disagreements, simply dismiss "good" in its ethical uses as itself being a confused, relativist term that has covert ideological functions, and, instead, for example, call the activities in question "productive" or "free" or "enterprising"? Anderson's reply is that in various areas of thought, particularly those embracing social or psychological issues, the prevalence of error frequently leads to ambiguities and misunderstandings in our use of language, but we do not on that account relinquish to the forces of confusion terms that do have a positive, empirical content (such as, "freedom" and its cognates), and so, then, with "good". Embedded in the continued use of the term throughout history has been an implicit recognition of its qualitative content, and even relativist conceptions like "duty" and "obligation" have carried with them a confused recognition of intrinsic goodness as one of the terms involved in these unspecified relations; in other words, in Anderson's view, the relativist, despite his confusions, does have some sense of goods as definite, qualitative activities and, indeed, it is because of this that his relativism gains greater plausibility. Accordingly, it is the job of ethical science to cut away the accretions and lay bare the positive goods that do exist.

Anderson does not, in support of his position, go into the etymology and history of the word "good", but it is worth remarking on the forceful view Nietzsche puts forward on this issue. According to him, the word "good" in various languages had its meaning debased in Christian times by being associated with a "slave morality" that was concerned principally with humility, sin, salvation and a denial of sexuality, and further misconstructions were made in more recent times when "good" was connected, especially by English moralists, with the ideas of altruism and usefulness. But its original and true meaning, Nietzsche maintains, is different. "Everywhere", he writes, " 'aristocrat', 'noble' (in the social sense), is the root idea, out of which have necessarily developed 'good' in the sense of 'with aristocratic soul', 'noble' in the sense of 'with a soul of high calibre', 'with a privileged soul'." [22] He allows that reference was often made to the socially superior position of the aristocrats, *but* in addition "good" referred to the possession of certain specific *traits* or *qualities* whoever happened to possess them. In line with this it may be noted that in Homeric Greek there was a word for "good" that had a clear descriptive force, conveying that someone good was "kingly, courageous and clever". [23]

Nietzsche may thus be interpreted as making a general plea for the reinstatement of the original positive sense of goodness,

[22] *The Genealogy of Morals*, trans. H.B. Samuel, J.N. Foulis, Edinburgh and London, 1910, pp. 22–23.
[23] Compare A.C. Macintyre, *A Short History of Ethics*, New York, Macmillan, 1966, p. 6.

and furthermore as offering a specific account of what qualities are good. On the latter question, while in some of his writings he has some obscure and perhaps dubious things to say, for example, about the aristocratic "master" or "overman", if we attend instead to his references to good men as being self-affirming, sincere, courageous, and *without* resentment or self-pity, we can see why Sorel in his account of "heroic values" was influenced by Nietzsche, and why there are affinities between Nietzsche's and Anderson's views on goodness. Compare, as a parallel with Nietzsche's contrast between true goodness and the values of Christianity, Anderson's observations on the criticism made by Joyce in *Ulysses* of the servile content of theology. "His 'free thought'," Anderson says, "consists, in the first instance, not in rejecting theology, but in taking it quite seriously. If there *were* a master of the universe, then Joyce, to the extent of his power, would fight against him; he will not endure servitude, he cannot accept sacrifice and atonement, he rebels against the low conception of life, the base morality, which they imply." (AM pp. 259–60)

Aside from etymology, Anderson's view about how people today learn to use the word "good" is that, occurring as it initially does in the child–parent situation, the process of learning the word is closely associated with what is emphasised by the Freudians: the retention or withdrawal of parental affection. The general effect of the parents' exhortations and admonitions "is to attach the notion of 'goodness' to something of which the child has direct experience", namely *love*.[24] After that it is a matter of circumstances whether a person's recognition of goodness will develop, in particular "whether love will be taken as the only good (the view the Freudians themselves tend to adopt) or merely as the first recognised or first strongly operative good". (S pp. 265–6) At any rate, it is Anderson's firm view that goodness *is* there to be recognised. Many people, he concedes, may be unconvinced by what he has to say about goodness, "but others

[24] Anderson takes it that our direct experience of love involves recognition of qualities as well as of relations. In his general philosophy he makes a distinction between "strict" or "pure" relations, which are straightforward spatio-temporal relations, and relations "in an extended sense" which, as well as being spatio-temporal relations, involve the presence of certain quite specific qualities. Thus, relations like *before, older than, above* or *near to* can hold between all sorts of things, but with, for example, *knows, employs, father of*, certain spatio-temporal relations obtain in each case but, as well, certain particular qualities are involved—only things of certain definite kinds can be knowers, employers or fathers—and likewise, then, to recognise the phenomenon of *love* is to recognise specific qualities as well as relations.

may see that it is something with which they have long been in certain ways acquainted". (S p. 267)

Ethics and Social Science

Anderson's view of the bearing of ethics on the study of society will be evident from the kind of position he advances. Ethics, being itself a positive science, is not a mere superfluous extra which may or may not obtain mention in the writings of social thinkers. On the contrary, it throws significant light on the complex ways of working of the phenomena that are, or need to be, studied by social science. Anderson, of course, would agree that most of what passes for ethical comment on socio-political matters is in fact an obstruction to scientific inquiry—compare those historians who take time off to praise or blame leading historical personages or who complain when this is not done, as was, for instance, notably illustrated a few years ago by the condemnations heaped on the English historian, A.J.P. Taylor, when he boldly suggested[25] that objective study of the causes of the last war was not in fact being furthered by the preoccupation historians have had with making moral judgements about Hitler. Historical writings which contain moral judgements of that kind, Anderson would say, are merely further examples of normative ethics, and their pronouncements about historical "villains"— apart from assuming individualism—are open to Croce's apt criticism about historical figures being "dragged in front of the tribunals of the pseudo-historians, stamped with a sentence and condemned to penalties of which we do not see how or where they are to be endured".[26]

Anderson, however, being concerned with ethics as an objective, non-prescriptive study of certain forms of human activity, can draw on that subject to deepen our understanding of social processes by making us aware of the ethical character of some of those processes. There is, for example, the way in which vital social or political struggles often involve the presence of good activities which are fighting for their existence against powerful inimical forces, or, again, the fact that the empirical nature of particular movements is affected by ethical factors, such as when "responsible participation in a productive movement is

[25] In his *The Origins of the Second World War*, London, H. Hamilton, 1961.
[26] *History as the Story of Liberty*, London, Allen and Unwin, 1941, p. 47.

marked by a diminution in the sense of guilt, by a rising above 'personal' values". (S p. 347) At the same time, recognition of what the social categories are is illuminated and reinforced by a study of positive ethics. Thus, ethical moralism, as we saw, is noted for its assumption of voluntarism, and likewise of social atomism, and also, especially under the influence of utilitarian moral theory, characteristically adopts "the solidarist conception of a total communal morality, a general virtue which gradually develops and brings welfare nearer and nearer". (S p. 243) So, in cutting through these moralist confusions to arrive at ethical realities, we are led once more to an affirmation of social determinism and, in particular, to a recognition of the ramifications of social pluralism.

SOCIAL PLURALISM

Contrast with Atomism and Solidarism

Anderson's social pluralism can now be expounded explicitly —as applying both to ethical and non-ethical features of social phenomena. By "social pluralism", as was briefly explained earlier, he understands a rejection of both social atomism and solidarism, that is, the term refers (1) to the existence of important social forces, like movements, in which individuals participate, and (2) to the plurality and complexity of such forces. His use of a single term in this context is due, not to a poverty of vocabulary, but to his sense of pluralism as an overall position interrelating a number of fundamental social truths. It is indeed possible to combine a rejection of social atomism with an assertion of solidarism—the Hegelian conception of society as an organic whole or unity is a celebrated example of such a partial pluralism —but in Anderson's view that kind of conception goes against the social facts which, instead, endorse a fully-fledged pluralism, the "two ways" of looking at which, as we may put it, embrace interwoven features of social complexes.

Against the solidarist assumption that society's existence depends on unity and harmony, Anderson points out that "the mere fact of opposition between different forms of organisation is not sufficient to establish social instability. On the contrary . . . a variety of organisations is a condition of social life, and among these, as well as within each, there will always be conflicting policies and competing demands".[27] Though there are interactions among them there is an irreducible plurality both of social activities and of mental tendencies, and this plurality, as

[27] "Political Freedom", *Zest*, No. 1, January 1932, p. 8.

is also disclosed by the ethical fact that good will never either triumph or totally disappear, is a permanent facet of history and society whether we are talking about "democracies" or other kinds of regimes. For "absolute totalitarianism is impossible" and "even in Russia and similarly in Germany", he wrote in the days of Stalin and Hitler, noting what later revelations corroborated, "there must be a certain variety and clash of interests". But also "pure democracy is equally impossible; there will never be a country in which freedom is established and guaranteed, in which certain interests do not have to struggle against repressive conditions". (PD p. 10)

Now the complexity of these divergent, competing social forces is manifested by the richness of their depth and detail and by the interplay between them. "We should think", for example, "of social movements not as formed by individuals but as passing through individuals, 'catching them up' as it were"; and "there may be a conflict within an individual between different adherences". (SS p. 4) Moreover, neither individuals nor the social forces and interests that work through them are unitary or compartmentalised. "The pluralistic view of society would ... be misconstrued if it were taken as affirming the existence of a number of fixed and separate interests, which could only be mechanically related to one another. It is clear that individuals may belong to many different institutions and movements, that even conflicting interests may be operative in him." (PD p. 9) We thus have to recognise the variegated, crisscrossing role in society of a number of factors that may be sorted out as follows: (1) institutions or organisations, notably the State, trade unions, political parties, big corporations, churches, educational bodies, (2) movements—political, scientific, artistic, religious—which are found inside and also outside of leading institutions, and (3) particular interests, outlooks or ways of life, including ones of a productive, enterprising, acquisitive, servile, and so on, kind that manifest themselves and struggle with one another within institutions and movements. Pluralism refers to the existence of these various factors or forces and to the affinities and conflicts between them.

Social Wholes or Complexes

Anderson thus adopts what some philosophers nowadays call a "holist" position (vis-à-vis what they call "methodological individualism"), but he himself does not use this expression and would have been disinclined to use it to describe his own position, because, in part, of its association with the work of Smuts who coined the term "holism" "to designate this fundamental factor operative towards the making or creation of wholes in the universe"[28] and used it to express a view of a markedly meta-physical and totalistic kind. Anderson strongly disclaims any suggestion of the Hegelian view that society, or the universe, forms a single ultimate whole and likewise the view of some "functionalists" in sociology and anthropology that society itself has some total function. "Social holism", then, is misleading because it can be, and is, used to describe (1) views of this monistic kind, and (2) qualified, pluralist views of social wholes of the type Anderson adopts, and for this reason the latter's view can be better described, for example, as one of "social complexism".

At any rate, on the issue of wholes and parts he takes up the general position that a whole is a complex phenomenon, the description of which is by no means exhausted by an enumeration of its parts, as the *interrelation* of the parts and the *qualities* of the whole and of the parts are also vitally involved. On the latter question of their qualities, while there are wholes the qualities of which are virtually identical with the qualities of their parts (a heap of sand or a sheet of metal are simple examples) there are also various wholes—the ones to which most significance is attached, he points out—that have certain specific qualities not possessed by their parts (a table or a tree, for instance). Anderson does not develop this subject in his social writings but it is easy to provide illustrations of his position in that area. In the case of a collection of people, for example, we may speak of this as a whole and of sub-collections of the same people as parts of this whole. Now very often such a whole and its parts will have very similar properties; if, say, the members of a lecture class, or a large public audience, or a street crowd, form such a whole, a half or even a tenth of the whole might still qualify as a class, an audience or a crowd. But under certain conditions even an amorphous whole of this kind may have distinct properties that would not attach to its sub-wholes; for example, we know that an address-followed-by-discussion meeting, given a certain size and a certain constellation of participants, may "fire" in a way that a smaller gathering would not have done, just as, in an historically important case, some of the Paris crowds of

---

[28] J.C. Smuts, *Holism and Evolution*, Macmillan, London, 1926, Chapter V.

1789–94 had a size and concentration that appears to have
created in them a highly distinctive atmosphere of revolutionary
élan that would have been lacking in smaller crowds. But the
relevant point, that social wholes may have important qualities
lacked by their sub-wholes, is more plainly evident when we
consider comparable but more complex collections of people.
Take, as one such example, armies; here, too, there can be some
sort of parallel with an ordinary crowd or audience in that,
for example, a small group of soldiers may march and drill
in the same way as a large number, or a regiment may even
reproduce the self-contained organisation of a whole army. But
these are obvious special cases, for normally in military matters
the distinction between greater and lesser wholes is marked by
sharp differences of quality and function. Without citing more
complicated examples, consider Napoleon's pithy observation,
referring to his Egyptian Campaign of 1798, that "If two Mamelukes are more than a match for three French soldiers, a thousand
French soldiers are more than a match for fifteen hundred
Mamelukes."

All the more evidently, the major "pluralistic wholes" on
which social science concentrates have certain properties which
their parts lack. Institutions, movements and ways of life, as
we have seen, are not mere aggregates of atomistic individuals;
also, however, they are not reducible to other social sub-wholes
(where coherence can be given to this conception) without loss
of significant properties. The State is one institution which has
some easily specifiable ingredient institutions—the executive,
parliament, judiciary, public service, army, etc.—but these are
certainly not a set of "sub-States". Or consider lesser institutions
like universities; suppose, to be fanciful, the members of some
Sydney university were all assembled on Bondi Beach one
morning. It is plain, quite apart from the missing role of law
and tradition—that is, the fact that pioneers or predecessors now
dead or graduates who have departed still affect a university—
that such a gathering of individuals would not reproduce the
complex features and relations of the university. Apart from such
ingredients as staff, students, administration and so on, that
institution contains within it various other forces and interests,
as Anderson points out in a passage which also displays his feeling
for the ethical factor:

> We have to take a pluralist view of the University as well
> as of society in general and to see that, within any so-called

academic institution, there are non-academic and anti-academic activities—that what is academic (for it is a question of movements and traditions, and not of "individuals") has to fight for survival against pseudo-academic Philistinism, as well as against the incult social mass, that the struggle of culture against "bourgeois society" exists also on the campus. (PA p. 5)

The question of sub-wholes or sub-complexes may have some complications here for, since inquiry and learning are activities commonly associated with universities, we may be tempted to maintain that if complexes of activities like these remained, and others like the forces opposed to inquiry or even the administrative apparatus totally disappeared, what survived would still qualify as a university. But that is a utopian speculation and Anderson, as a social realist, takes it that universities are, and are very likely to remain, *at best* (from the point of view of inquiry) institutions of the kind he outlines, and in that case, then, some of their most distinctive features are in no sense reproduced in their parts.

Comparable observations can be made about other leading institutions and about such social forces or associations as movements, causes and ways of life, though in these cases it is sometimes more difficult to give content to the conception of their ingredients or sub-divisions. Movements, on which Anderson places considerable stress, may be described as unformalised or unarticulated engagements of people in the pursuit of some end or common cause that have a force or power of their own, including that of being able to spark off support from, or communicate esprit de corps to, actual or potential adherents. But there is a certain indefiniteness attaching to the term because movements extend over a range of cases—they may be wide-scale movements that are forerunners of formal or legal parties or organisations, but may also, in a more nebulous way, be virtually identical with causes or with ways of life. At any rate, if we take, for example, such disparate cases as the labour movement, say, in Australia in the 1890s, the Impressionist and Post-Impressionist movements in painting, the temperance movement, the women's liberation movement, the cause of freedom of thought, the republican cause in Australia today, or again, productive, acquisitive or servile outlooks or ways of life, it is clear that we have in each case a genuine social phenomenon and one whose key features are not exhibited or reproduced in its parts or phases. This is true too when we can coherently speak about ingredient movements or sub-movements; for instance, given a schism in a religious—or a political or an intellectual—movement, the standard outcome is the formation of two or more new movements none (or not more than one) of which can be equated with the original movement.

In fine, then, the social forces described by Anderson are "holistic" in the sense, and no more than this, that they are social wholes or, better, social complexes, each of which has certain characteristic ways of working not possessed by any social sub-complexes into which they can be divided or analysed.

Social and Psychological Factors

A significant related question Anderson does take up, albeit briefly, is that of the place of *psychological* vis-à-vis *social* processes in social and ethical inquiry. In line with his realism and empiricism, he maintains, of course, that mental and social factors are equally real but in one of his key discussions of ethics we find the following passage: "Goods, we may say, are those mental activities, or those social activities, which are 'free' or enterprising, which exhibit the spirit of enterprise. It might be better to come down on the mental side. The main point is that ethics penetrates both the psychological and the sociological field, but is nevertheless a distinct and positive inquiry." (S p. 267) Now a member of Anderson's "school", W.H.C. Eddy, in the course of a valuable discussion of ethico-social questions, queries Anderson's suggestion that primacy be given to the mental side and maintains instead "that it is not 'better to come down on the mental side' but that we have to come down on both and see that certain social activities are part of the field of ethics (as the whole of the rest of Anderson's argument appears to me to indicate) and that these social activities are ways of life, movements or moralities". [29] The issue here, it is true, is about *ethics*, but Eddy's point I regard as well taken. It is rather curious that Anderson should display this wavering towards the psychological side. Some support for it could perhaps be offered by contending that, while individual minds and communities resemble each other in being pluralistic complexes, in any of which there are divisive and repressive activities as well as communicative, enterprising and spontaneous

---

[29] "Ethics and Politics", *A.J.P.P.*, September 1944, p. 74.

ones, nevertheless the latter activities are stronger or more pervasive in *minds* in which goods flourish vis-à-vis *communities* in
which goods flourish. But against that, if instead of whole communities we consider *movements* and *ways of life*, certain of these are
surely, in Anderson's view, no less characterised by communica-
tiveness and the like than are certain minds. Another argument for
giving some sort of primacy to mental factors might be advanced
by placing more emphasis in Anderson's account of goods on the
creative aspects of scientific, artistic and other productive movements for that would bring into the foreground the psychological
question of the presence in certain individuals of creative talents
and the like—but that would be at the expense of his usual
emphasis on the co-operative and communicative features of the
movements to which these individuals belong. Anderson himself,
however, does not offer any explanations of this kind and, as
Eddy points out, the whole tenor of his stated argument goes
the other way.

Moreover, when in a later discussion Anderson refers to the
same issues in relation to *social science* he certainly does not "come
down on the mental side". "There is no question", he says, "of
social processes having a reality inferior to that of psychological
processes; indeed, if we are to give any serious account of a
man's life, we must present the interrelation (including the clash)
of forms of activity in which he and others participate—of which
he is a 'vehicle' rather than an initiator." (RA p. 162) What
he calls "forms of activity" are in fact firmly grounded in both
the social and psychological fields. To speak of men's participation
in forms of activity is the same as speaking of their participation
in social movements, or causes, or ways of life, while on the
psychological side it is "forms of activity that make up 'individuals'". (RA p. 162) Of course, the science of psychology is
different from the science of society, the former encompassing
all the psychological activities going on in men only some of
which may have social importance; nevertheless, there are
psychological activities with which social science is vitally concerned, these being, as Anderson puts it, any such activity which
is "a constituent in a wider movement (one passing through
many persons)". (S p. 343) There may be some difficulty in
understanding clearly Anderson's position on this question owing
to a comparative vagueness in his—and ordinary—language
which could probably be best met by coining new and more
precise terms, as, in general, a furtherance of Anderson's contribution to social science would require. But short of doing that,

it would be of some help to speak in a more cumbersome but plainer way about "psycho-social" (or "socio-psychological") activities, "psycho-social" movements, and so on, thus making it clear that these real, but little attended to, forms of activity cut across both the mental and social arenas.

The importance Anderson attaches to the interpenetration of mental, social and ethical phenomena leads him, when he considers the question of important contributors to social thought, to pay careful attention to the work of Freud, as well as of Marx. "Freud's work", he notes in one tribute, "has given a tremendous impetus to rigorous thinking on human affairs, to the establishment of a real psychological science ... Freudianism will remain as one of the determinants of all critical thinkers." (S p. 362) But while Freud's insistence on determinism in the human field and his elaboration of the conflicts between repressive and other human tendencies are also valuable contributions to the field of social study, unfortunately his specific writings in that field— notably *Civilization and its Discontents*—are open to obvious criticism. Thus, Anderson points out, while he also takes no account "of the variety and conflict of the institutions which may be said to constitute a civilisation, it is in regard to the other 'unit', the individual on whom civilisation is supposed to impinge, that Freud is most seriously in error; it is his individualism that wrecks his social theory". (S p. 341) Similarly, "the doctrine of 'ego, id and super-ego' which finally emerged, and which now dominates the work of the Freudian school, was largely a reinstatement of individualistic or atomistic thinking" (S p. 369)— though Anderson elsewhere makes the interesting suggestion that that doctrine could be improved by arguing that "the distinction between ego, id and super-ego is a distinction, not among mental 'instances' or organisations, but among possible ways of acting of the same mental tendency (the same passion, as we may put it in default of any more neutral term)". (S p. 346) So Freud's social insights are only scattered ones; his work "shows that he has no conception of social forces, that he is endeavouring all the time to reduce them to personal (or psychological) terms, and thus that he is directly opposed to all that is valuable in Marxism" (*A.H.* 1937, p. 139)—and it remains Marx (despite his own shortcomings, including lack of appreciation of psychology) who lays firm foundations for the study of social pluralism.

MARX AND MARXISM

Anderson, in his first decade in Australia, 1927–1937, was sympathetic first to orthodox Communism and then to Trotskyism and so accepted to a considerable extent both Marxist and Communist theories. This means that there is an important difference between his early views on Marxist social theory and his subsequent assessment of it. But his early acceptance of Marx's view of classes and economic forces and of Lenin's view of the U.S.S.R. will be set aside for treatment in Part II where Anderson's development will be traced, and what will be discussed here will be his maturer judgement on the work of Marx and his followers, which he first wrote about detail in 1935 and which, like the other parts of his social philosophy so far discussed, he adhered to thereafter. It should be noted, too, that even in the early phase of his political thought he does not, in the usual Communist Party way, merely repeat what Marx, Lenin, or others say, but has his own characteristic and independent ways of formulating issues which pointed the way to his later position—as when, for instance, in an early defence of revolution, he speaks of "the clash of social forces" and "the struggle for existence among these forces, or as we may put it, among types of social organisation";[30] or when he emphasises the question of the *political freedom* of the working class and advocates their "general participation in the framing and carrying out of policies". (FC p. 7) Moreover, while he did at that time sometimes speak of social change in a way that fits in with the Marxist view of "dialectic jumps"—compare his comment "It may be said of any such thing, and not merely of society, that it passes through various stages, each marked by some sort of struggle which

[30] "Evolution and Revolution", *W.W.*, 15 July 1927.

culminates in a more or less abrupt transition to the next stage"
(*T.C.* December 1927 p. 13)—at no time did he give credence
to the metaphysical theory of the dialectic or to related theories
about truth and knowledge, all of which are utterly at variance
with his realism and empiricism.

Marxist Philosophy

"The history of philosophy is the philosophy of history", Hegel
claims in one of his aphorisms, and an analogous running together,
if not identification, of philosophical with social and historical
questions is found in the work of Karl Marx. That is why it is
important to distinguish between his general philosophy and his
social philosophy and to appraise the two separately, because—so
Anderson's judgement runs—the former impedes the latter and
"a refutation of the philosophy can only advance the most
typically Marxist contributions to science". (S p. 293) In this
connection, though, while in referring to "Marxist" views
Anderson often makes no distinction between Marx himself and
"the Marxists"—by whom he understands primarily Engels,
Kautsky, Lenin, Trotsky and orthodox Russian Communists—he
sometimes does distinguish between the two, especially in the
case of philosophy. The problem here, of course, arises from the
fact that Marx did not fully and systematically set out his position,
least of all in the field of general philosophy, so that in this area,
in particular, he may be exonerated from the worst confusions
of his followers. Thus, while in Anderson's view, Marx "contributed notably" to the philosophical criticisms of dualism,
atomism and rationalistic ethics (RA pp. 165–66), his philosophy
was not sufficiently worked out and "it was left to men of inferior
intelligence, like Engels, or men like Lenin for whom philosophy
was of merely incidental interest, to supply the missing doctrines".
(S p. 292)

We have, then, in Marx's work and that of his followers, an
entanglement of socio-philosophical questions in which, as various
writers have pointed out,[31] there is a tension or conflict between
incompatible elements which, in Anderson's preferred terminology, involve on the one hand rationalism, monism and relativism,

---

[31] Compare, in particular, Max Eastman, whose works, *Marx, Lenin and the Science of
Revolution*, London, Allen and Unwin, 1926, and *The Last Stand of Dialectic Materialism*,
New York, Polemic Publishers, 1934, present numerous arguments with which Anderson
agrees. He is, however, critical of Eastman for making certain concessions to voluntarism.

and on the other hand, empiricism, pluralism and an objective treatment of social and other issues. This conflict stems in large part from the survival in Marxist thought of Hegelian monistic and dialectic metaphysics. Hegel—whose thought Anderson was steeped in as a student in Glasgow University—he regards as making a fundamental contribution to social philosophy "in his rejection of social atomism and his recognition of institutions" (S p. 323), but his overall philosophy of the Absolute or Whole which is supposed to overcome, unify and make intelligible the diversity of its moments or parts, is a rationalist theory of an ultimate, all-inclusive reality and as such is open to philosophical refutation. Standard arguments advanced by Anderson against monism turn on the fact that the monist cannot state and argue for his position without assuming independence and difference. He may, by trading in identities and ambiguities, try to make his position plausible, but criticism proceeds by exposing these identities and ambiguities. Thus, it may be said that when "A is not B" A is also somehow identical with B, but in that case, Anderson points out, "we could not distinguish between affirmative and negative propositions, or indeed make statements at all". (S p. 42) Likewise, when Hegelians tell us that differences are comparatively unreal, the reply is this: "that if we say that differences are comparatively unreal, then 'the comparative unreality of differences' *is* ultimately real. Yet it is not *the* ultimately real or Absolute; it must be an aspect or expression of the Absolute. But, in taking this view, we are admitting that it is *really different* from other aspects or expressions." (S pp. 47–48) The case against all ontological monisms Anderson summarises in one passage as follows:

> A monist must deny all change and all differentiation; the One can have no history and no parts. For to say that it has a part is to assert the existence of the situation "X is a part of the One", to assert, that is, the equal presence of X and the One in this situation and thus to take the One as simply one thing among others and no longer the totality of things ... the One, however it may be characterised (strictly speaking it cannot be characterised at all ...), is incompatible with history and plurality; and the only resort is the assertion of a thorough-going pluralism, the denial of a "universe" or totality of things, and the recognition of the existence anywhere and at any time of a heterogeneity of things. (S p. 306)

I have spent time on these arguments, which also elucidate Anderson's philosophical pluralism, because of the vital bearing they have on his criticisms of part of the Marxist position. Thus, a fundamental difficulty with that position, Anderson points out, is that a number of its characteristic formulations imply a similar untenable monism. Marx claims, for example, that Hegel's philosophy "must be turned right side up again, if you would find the rational kernel within the mystical shell",[32] but when he and Engels (not to mention their candidly monist follower, Plekhanov) speak in a monistic way of *determination* by productive forces and relations, of the *inevitable* developments that they can predict, of *contradictions* in things (for example, capitalism) being overcome and made *rational*, and so on, they are committed to much more than a scientific or empirical rewriting of Hegel's dialectic monism of Spirit. "The only serious answer," Anderson argues, "to the assertion that the universe is spiritual, is that there is not a universe. If all things were aspects of the One, the One could just as much, though just as little, be called mental as anything else. Hence any doctrine of 'the physical universe', any 'materialistic monism', can no more provide an answer to Hegel than any form of atomism can." (S p. 85) But such a definite, non-monistic answer is missing from the work of Marx and his followers. Marx claims that in his theory the "dialectic" is freed from the mystifications of Hegel, but it is "as much a mystification in the one theory as in the other" (S p. 306), and though Spirit is replaced by Matter, Marxists still assume, sometimes overtly and sometimes covertly, a position of ontological monism. "The root of the confusion," Anderson sums it up, "is the doctrine of a 'primary reality'" (*A.H.* 1936 p. 194), and it is the "conception of reality, society, humanity, advancing *as a whole*, that prevents the working out of a necessarily pluralistic theory of the struggle of organisations". (S p. 324) It is a patent misconstruction of the issues about monism if they are merely taken to involve a clash of beliefs over what is the "stuff" or "substance" of reality; there is a similar otiose ontology whether the primary or ultimate reality is supposed to be Hegel's Absolute Spirit or, instead, *materiality*,—or whether, as Anderson interestingly suggests Marx really implies, it is supposed that "all reality is social reality". (RA p. 159)

---

[32] Karl Marx, *Capital*, London, Lawrence and Wishart, 1972. Afterword to the Second German Edition.

A related, more explicit Marxist doctrine, inherited from Hegel and criticised by Anderson, concerns *truth*. In the Hegelian system of monism there are not only degrees of reality—measured, it is claimed by degree of approximation to Absolute Reality—but also corresponding degrees of truth; that is, all truths are supposed to be only "partial" or "relative", each proposition having a greater or less degree of truth according to the extent to which it embodies, or approximates to, ultimate truth as manifested in the Whole or Absolute. Within Marxism this view reappears particularly in the crude "class view of truth",—which is backed up by the monistic view of historical materialism, according to which all ideas or beliefs are derivative superstructure reflections of the material base and have only a dependent, relative claim to truth.

Anderson, in a variety of references to truth in his writings, draws attention to the confused logic of those who try to deny or obscure objective consideration of issues, and he is easily able to reveal the confusions of the Marxist view. For example, "the raising of the question, in regard to any social view, 'Is this proletarian?' or 'Is this Marxist?' instead of 'Is this true?'" involves "the obscurantist conceptions of points of view and relative truths". (OF p. 12) It depends on the kind of evasion of the issue in which the origins or effects of a view are considered, but not the view itself. Marxists, moreover, have a penchant for another well-known fallacy, the argument from authority, as is illustrated by their attempts to substantiate views merely by quoting from Marxist texts; their "dialectic" procedure of selecting passages from the texts that happen to suit them is likewise invalid—as Anderson puts it, "if a statement of Marx, or Lenin, lends support to some view of the 'dialectician', it is true because it is Marxist; if it is opposed to his view, it was merely meant to 'apply' at the time when it was made". (OF p. 12)

In addition to employing these obviously fallacious forms of reasoning, Marxists are subject to some basic philosophical confusions about truth. These confusions have been exposed at various times in the history of philosophy, but the key error can be illustrated by the following criticism of Hegelian idealists. According to them we cannot assert mere relative truths in isolation, we must assert them in the context of Absolute Reality: thus (1) "A is B" can't be asserted on its own, it really amounts to (2) "Reality is such that A is B". But in that case, Anderson points out, (2) really amounts to (3) "Reality is such that Reality is such that A is B", and so on forever; in other words, we have a vicious infinite regress that reveals we are involved in a contradiction. The way out of the contradiction is to recognise that we can assert (2) without asserting (3), but in that case we can equally assert the ordinary proposition (1) "A is B" on its own—for "if we can understand and accept the second proposition without further 'reference', the same applies to the first". (S p. 116) As this criticism helps to disclose, the critic of objective truth has to *assume* that truth in order to communicate his own beliefs, whether these are beliefs about truths or about other things.

Likewise, then, the social relativist, such as the Marxist, cannot coherently substantiate his claims about the relativity of truth. Thus, when he tells us what his theory is by making statements like "All truths are relative to class position" or "All beliefs are ideologically distorted" he has to maintain (contrary to what he is trying to say) that *these* statements are objectively true—and he similarly understands to be objectively true typical *specific* statements he makes, such as "There are classes that conflict with one another", "Belief X is a bourgeois belief", "Belief Y is a proletarian belief". Or, as a different example, take Marx's statement that "Theory becomes realised in a people only in so far as it is the realisation of its needs." As Anderson comments, "If Marx means that a people thinks what it needs to think, still it does think that and think it true. If he means that it thinks that something is what it needs, again the question is whether that *is* what it needs." (S p. 316) Or, again, consider Engels' well-known attempt to argue for the "relative truth" of Boyle's law concerning how the volume of a gas varies in relation to the pressure to which it is subjected. Regnault discovered that the law does not apply in certain cases, and Engels maintains that Boyle's law is not false, instead it is "approximately correct", "true within specific bounds", but not "absolute, a final truth of last instance within specific bounds". Anderson points out that Engels' argument, evasive though it is, does not succeed in explaining away questions about objective truth. He has, for example, to assume at the very least that some gases *do* and some gases *do not* have the properties Boyle described, otherwise we should not understand what Engels is talking about. And so far as Boyle's law is concerned, it is—and was—*false*, though the belief in it may have been *useful*. Regnault showed the law to be false, Anderson points out, but also "that *all gases within specific bounds* have the property X. In other words, a *different* proposition is true, not relatively but absolutely; it is not that a certain proposition has limited truth but that a limited subject has, absolutely, a certain predicate." (S p. 297)

One other aspect of Marxist philosophy of which Anderson is sharply critical is its adherence to a representative theory of knowledge. He refers particularly to Lenin who, largely following Engels, wrote at length on the subject. Lenin wants a theory of knowledge which, he says, does not go beyond "'the naive realism' of any healthy person who has not been an inmate of an insane asylum or a pupil of the idealist philosophers" and wants to adopt the materialist view that "outside us, and independently of us, there exist objects, things, bodies and that our perceptions are images of the external world".[33] But as this last clause reveals, Lenin, though striving to be realistic, in fact falls back on a Lockean representational theory—which incidentally involves him and Engels in Locke's passive, *tabula rasa* view of the mind or knower, thus neglecting its active, dynamic role which Marx himself (in Anderson's view correctly) follows Hegel in emphasising. Any theory which maintains that what we know are "ideas", "images", "reflections", "copies", "pictures" or "photographs" (as Lenin even says) and that these represent or correspond to outside things, is open to formidable objections. Thus, to mention briefly three of Anderson's criticisms, (1) if what we know are "ideas" or "pictures", it is inexplicable why we should come to suppose that there are outside things at all; for example, when Marxists claim that "picturing" is verified by practice, this can only mean we verify one picture by reference to another picture and they are quite unable to say "how the passage from one to the other gives us any knowledge of what is not a picture". (*A.H.* 1936 p. 193) In fact, (2) "in order to show that 'an idea' is a good or bad copy of 'an external thing', we should have to know them both and compare them—but, of course, if we can know external things directly, then the whole picture theory collapses". (S pp. 299–300) In any case, (3) when it is supposed that we cannot have direct knowledge of external things but can only know them through intermediary "ideas" or "pictures", the contradiction emerges that, in accordance with the same reasoning, we cannot know a "picture" directly, but only "a picture of a picture", and so on, and the way out of this vicious regress lies in the recognition that we are not required to have recourse

---

[33] V.I. Lenin, *Materialism and Empirio-Criticism*, Moscow, Progress Publishers, 1964, pp. 55 and 88.

to intermediaries, but have direct knowledge of external things themselves.

Marxist philosophy is thus subject to a variety of confusions, but, despite this, it is, in Anderson's judgement, on the right philosophical track in recognising such things as causal determination, the existence of independent, non-mental occurrences, and above all "that all things are events or processes interacting with other processes". (S p. 311)

Theory of Society

Moving from general to social philosophy, Anderson takes it that the work of Marx and his followers makes a much more substantial and original contribution to knowledge in the latter field, but here too, he argues, there are negative as well as positive ingredients in Marxist thought so that the careful student has the task of disentangling genuine contributions to science from persisting socio-philosophical confusions. Thus, Marx's "doctrine of social struggles throughout history" lays the foundation of "a materialism of a non-totalistic kind" (RA p. 161), but there is, in the vital conception of historical materialism as ordinarily presented by Marxists, an unresolved tension between monistic and pluralistic elements that has been noted by a variety of critics and commentators.[34] Thus, according to Marx's most famous statement of his position, there is an economic "base" or "foundation" on which arises a "superstructure" (1) of political and legal forms and (2) of ideas or ideologies. That, however, is a metaphorical formulation which, taken seriously, implies that economic factors have a priority, including a *temporal* priority, over superstructural factors, and that is a view that pluralists forcibly criticise. Anderson's way of making the point is by objecting to the claim made by Engels—in expounding Marx—"that human beings must have food and drink, clothing and shelter, *first of all*, before they can interest themselves in politics, science, art, religion, and the like", and "that these latter must be

---

[34] Compare, for example, Eastman's comment on the theory of economic determinism, "A theory which ignores the difference between the verbs *condition* and *determine* cannot be called scientific", *Marx, Lenin and the Science of Revolution*, p. 51; and Pareto's verdict that we must distinguish between the "popular" and the "learned" interpretations of historical materialism, the former being quite erroneous because "it consists in explaining everything by the economic conditions of a people", while the latter, less narrow view, presents us with an "objective and scientific conception of history", *Les Systèmes Socialistes*, 3rd ed., Vol. II, Geneva, Droz, 1965, p. 386.

explained out of the former".[35] "This", Anderson insists, "is glaringly false. It is not the case that the winning of subsistence is antecedent to cultural ideas and activities; it is, for the most part, bound up with them and is frequently postponed or subordinated to them (that is, men risk their subsistence for the sake of their 'ideas')." (S p. 330) Or, as he puts it in the specific case of art, the interest in artistic matters "is an independent *interest* ... which, however slight its social effects may be and however it may be affected by other interests and social conditions, is not 'subsidiary' to anything".[36] In other words, superstructural factors are *not* reducible to or explicable by economic ones—not even "ultimately" or "in the last resort" for that kind of hedging merely reinstates covertly the original monism. There may indeed be variations in quantity or strength and in the relative interaction among, for example, economic, political, scientific, artistic, ethical and religious activities—it may be, for instance, that the first two are more powerful or influential social agents than the others—but each activity, though affected by other social conditions, exists in its own right as a substantial, independent form of social activity.

If the narrow economic theory of historical materialism has to be expanded to accommodate other social forces, there is a related need to modify, in a pluralist way, standard Marxist doctrines about classes, ideologies and the State. Anderson, while acknowledging the positive contribution made by Marx to the theory of organisations and of social conflicts, regards his class theory as defective on two connected counts. First, there is the fact that Marx himself is not exempt from individualism. This is revealed, for instance, by his use of "the language of individualistic utilitarianism" (S p. 323), that is, by his concentration on talk about the *wills*, *ends* and *needs* of the persons who make up the classes and about the struggle between these persons, instead of referring to classes themselves as types of social forces which conflict with one another and in which individuals participate or are immersed. Similarly, it is worth observing, Anderson voices criticism of Lenin for being atomistic in his conception of the professional revolutionist—on the ground that such a revolutionist is not a participant in the regular institutions of the country that he is supposed to help liberate and Lenin mistakenly sees

---

[35] "Speech at the Graveside of Karl Marx", Marx and Engels, *Selected Works*, Vol. 3, Moscow, Progress Publishers, 1970, p. 162.

[36] *Some Questions in Aesthetics*, published by the Sydney University Literary Society, 1932, p. 9.

him as an agent who, in coming from outside, can contrive or control the course of events. Second, there is the exiguity of Marx's view of economic classes which leads to a playing down of the *variety* of social conflicts and to a failure to recognise the complex array of organisations and movements which, as we have seen, Anderson takes to be fundamental parts of the social structure. This weakness, moreover, he maintains in a characteristic criticism of Communist Marxists, helps to explain the transition activists of that kind so often make from liberalism to illiberalism.

> The doctrine of "class rule" is rooted in failure to comprehend the multiplicity and the interplay of social interests, yet its adherents are commonly actuated in the first instance by a desire for the liberation of the oppressed. The initial simplification of social affairs, however, treating them all as manifestations of a single conflict (that of "capital" and "labour"), leads straight to the imposition of uniformity and the exercise of a tyranny just as vicious as any that was originally attacked. (PD p. 10)

Correspondingly in need of criticism is the theory of *ideologies*, according to which, as a consequence of the simple ideas-as-superstructure view of intellectual activity, beliefs are mere dependent reflections of the economic base. Interwoven with this view is the "relative" or "class" conception of truth, Anderson's criticism of which has already been outlined. Contrary to the superstructure or reflection view of beliefs, the truth or falsity of a belief is not determined by its origins or effects. It is a form of *ignoratio elenchi* for example, to judge a proposition to be false (or true) on the basis of the class position of the person asserting the proposition. It is indeed the case, Anderson argues, that the occurrence of scientific beliefs no less than the occurrence of illusory beliefs is subject to social conditions and these conditions are open to investigation, but in order to decide whether believed propositions are true or false, independent reference must be made to what it is that those propositions actually assert.

There are, however, some complexities attaching to Marx's view of ideology. While he was responsible for the crude "reflection" view of ideologies outlined above, which is the one reproduced by most of his followers, he himself at times suggests a different, more defensible view according to which an ideology is not any belief (or any set of beliefs), or even any social belief, but a *special type* of socially influential belief which, though sincerely believed by many of its adherents, (1) is *false* or *absurd* and (2) has a *distorting* or *mystifying* social role, for example, that of covertly promoting the interests of a ruling class. Marx himself, in fact, used the *word* "ideology" only in this latter sense, that is, in a *derogatory* way, and while even then he confined his view to *class* ideologies, it is easy to see how it can be extended in a pluralist manner to refer to the ideological beliefs of more ramified groups or movements.[37]

Now, so far as Anderson is concerned, he has little to say specifically about ideology and indeed in his relatively few uses of that term he mostly follows Lenin (as distinct from Marx) in referring indifferently to proletarian, bourgeois, and so on, ideology, that is, to any set of related political beliefs. In a late essay, however, he does refer to ideology in Marx's special sense, connecting it with his own account of *relativist* thinking. (RA pp. 165–66) But aside from use of the term, if we take the valuable part of Marx's view of ideology to be his conception of the unmasking or demystification of prevalent but illusory social beliefs, then it is plain that much of Anderson's social commentary consists in making that kind of criticism—compare, in addition to his criticisms of relativism in ethics (a potent source of ideology in Marx's special sense), his recurrent emphasis on rejection of *fetishes* associated, for example, with patriotism and religion, and his general concern with *the exposure of illusions*.

In the Marxist view the State, as a political institution, is another part of the dependent social superstructure, or, in class terms, is merely the "executive committee" of the ruling economic class. Anderson at one time endorsed this "theory of the State as the organ of class domination" (T.C. February 1928 p. 10), but soon abandoned that view in favour of a pluralist position critical of Marxism. Thus, he sees the State as having a definite function "as adjuster of differences, or as the general machinery of adjustment" (PD p. 8), though there is no "pure" or "impartial" adjustment that is effected by the State—that is, he agrees with the Marxists in rejecting the conventional bourgeois claim that the State is an organ of reconciliation that rationally and fairly arbitrates among competing social interests. The important point is that the State is no mere social "instrument" but an independent force with special interests of its own. (Compare, as a parallel, Anderson's conception of the psychological *ego* as something which "adjudicates", but not "impartially", among rival mental

---

[37] Compare A.J. Baker, "Ideologies", *Libertarian*, published by the Libertarian Society at Sydney University, No. 2, 1958.

forces or passions, and does so by being a force or passion in its own right.) Now, in the Marxist corpus there is a guarded suggestion of this viewpoint in references made by Engels and Lenin to the State's having the role of softening or covering up antagonisms between classes, and in Marx's conception of "Bonapartism", that is, of the State—as in France under Louis Bonaparte—temporarily raising itself above the contending classes. But that, Anderson holds, is an insight into the realities of the State which is irreconcilable with the other, instrument-of-the-ruling-class view, for it entails recognition of the fact that the State is, after all, an institution with independent ways of working of its own. In other words, Anderson's position is in line with that of various other critics of Marxism—including students of the operation of States taken over and controlled by Communists—according to which, contrary to the general Marxist underestimation of political factors, the State apparatus and its attendant bureaucracy, etc., is a powerful social force in its own right. Or, in the words of a writer influenced by Anderson's social theory: "Political institutions are not just instruments themselves. They influence the character of political activities and decisions. This holds, first, of the institution of State power altogether ('all power corrupts') ... However strong other influences, say economic tendencies, may be, there is no doubt that State power has a role of its own, has tendencies of its own which 'catch up' those who arrive at it."[38]

Determinism and Social Planning

A fundamental part of Marxism that Anderson trenchantly criticises is its view of "social engineering", which, he notes, is closely associated with the confusion of theory with policy, that is, of issues about what is the case with issues about what is to be done, and, further, with the metaphysical assumption that the proletarian revolution "has 'history'" or indeed "the *universe* on its side". (S p. 311) If the last suggestion represents a survival of Hegelian monism in Marxist thought, the fact is, Anderson argues, that even in his socio-empirical moments, Marx's theory of social determinism and prediction is essentially a monistic one; it is that which convinces him—and many other would-be "social

[38] R. Rhees, "'Social Engineering'", *Mind*, 1947, p. 324; also in his *Without Answers*, London, Routledge and Kegan Paul, 1969, p. 59.

controllers"—of the feasibility of his plans for large-scale "social engineering". But, Anderson insists, this belief ignores the abiding presence of uncontrolled and unintended consequences of human interventions and, in fact, is one more example of the voluntarist outlook. "The attempt to bind the future", he expresses it, "is an attempt to get out of history; it is a denial of social and political law, of the operation of things independently of what anyone might desire." (DI p. 16)

The vital issue thus turns on the exact view we must take of social or historical determinism, prediction and "control" and here Anderson, while upholding determinism, distinguishes sharply between a pluralist and a monistic conception of it. In line with other philosophical critics he recognises that various confusions are rife concerning "causal chains", and the like, which are supposed to be involved by determinism, and argues that there is no such thing as a causal chain or transitive causality any more than there is a single, *the* future. Accordingly, in rejecting these monistic conceptions "we are recognising that there is no unilinear form of development but interaction at all points". (S p. 134) As P.H. Partridge points out in elaborating this kind of position, there is no single, self-enclosed causal series; in any given case there is "a collision, or intersection, of two independent lines of development", and "there is no *single* factor to explain why each process should have reached just that phase at any time".[39]

The kind of position Anderson contests and his reasons for doing so, can be helpfully illustrated by what he has to say against Freud as well as Marx. Thus, according to Freud, the primary causal factors affecting human beings are their original, infantile characteristics, and against this Anderson's argument, which needs to be quoted at length to capture its precise force, runs as follows:

> But actual development is conditioned by both character and circumstances, and is not a function of either. It may be true that only things of the sort X ever become Y, but also true that this happens only when an X comes under the influence of C. There is, then, no more sense in saying that the acquired character Y was *in* the original character X than in saying that it was in C; to say that it was there "potentially" is only a way of denying the fact in question, that, when X is subjected to C, *something new* appears. Thus it is a plain fact of human history that many types of activity do not arise at all until later life, and to say that their

---

[39] "Contingency", *A.J.P.P.*, 1938, especially pp. 9–14.

potentiality, their basis, that out of which they come, must
have been present in infancy is really to deny interaction.
(S p. 353)

Marx and his followers, Anderson likewise argues, are equally
unwilling to accept interactions, even though they give primacy
to "outside" circumstances instead of the "inside" characteristics
stressed by the Freudians. That is, contrary to the Marxist assumption that "a thing's history is determined entirely by the influence
of outside things, as if they could act, but it could not", what we
actually have is "the interrelation of independent forces including
those *within* a given thing". (*A.H.* 1938 p. 14) A concrete example
is the Marxist doctrine of "shortening the birth pangs" (of revolutionary change), with which is associated the dictum "Freedom
is consciousness of necessity" which some Marxists have taken
over from Hegel in an attempt to show that human beings cannot
alter the "direction" of social change, though they can "accel-
erate" or "delay" its coming about. But here the pluralist point
is that the notion that human knowledge of necessary laws can
have some *influence* carries with it the assumption that by knowing
the laws we can intervene and affect them—so that the laws are
not after all inexorable, or there is not just a *single* outcome,
contrary to what is assumed by the Marxists.

The correct view of determinism, then, is pluralist, not monist,
and from this flows a falsification of the grandiose claims made
by Marxists and others about "scientific" social planning. There
are two major pluralist objections to these claims, one concerning
prediction and one concerning human control of social phenomena. Thus, first, while prediction is certainly possible in the social
field, there is no question of "total" or "overall" prediction.
"Our predictions", Anderson sums it up, "must be based not
only on a knowledge of certain 'general laws' but on the recognition of certain 'collocations'." (S p. 310) Expanding this, when
we do have knowledge of a "law" or universal proposition, (1)
"all A are B", and the fact (2) that "X is A", then, of course,
we can correctly predict that "X will be B". But there are many
cases where we lack knowledge of the appropriate laws and/or
particular social situations. But given a law for the sake of argument, can't we make some predictions? And furthermore, if we
don't already know that "X is A", what about predicting *that*
and hence, with the law, predicting "X will be B"? The answer
is that given the law, on its own, all we can do is make the hypothe-
tical prediction that "If X is A then it will be B". To make an
actual prediction soundly we need to have the further information

that "X is or will be A", and so far as predicting this in turn is concerned we cannot predict it solely on the strength of our knowledge of (1) "all A are B"—to assume that we can somehow do so is again to assume that we have an inevitable, single line of development that does not interact with other independent series of events. To predict with reason that "X will be A" we need *further* information, say that there is (3) a further law, "All C are A" and that in fact (4) "X is C", and so far as predicting (4) in turn is concerned, we again need further independent information, and so on in every case. But if, conversely, some of the relevant knowledge is lacking, then we will be in no position to make the requisite predictions.

Furthermore, as the second crucial objection to "scientific" social planning, whatever actual predictions we can make, it is a confusion to believe that we have *control* over the phenomena involved. As against the view that "we are to find out laws of sociology in order to change society", Anderson argues that in fact "in finding out laws, we are finding out what *cannot* be helped". (S pp. 351–52) An example he mentions is that of recurrent "agitations for peace". Suppose, instead of the airing by publicists of the view that there must be a way of achieving this desired goal, a scientific attempt was successfully made "to determine the objective conditions . . . of the occurrence of inter-national conflicts", then Anderson suggests, it is exceedingly likely that these conditions would be such as to preclude long-lasting peace—and in that case the predictions that could be made would show that the desired anti-war outcomes were simply not possible. Or, as another kind of example, consider those cases where human intervention may in part, or at first, implement intended social consequences but—as notoriously happens with attempts to guarantee full employment, introduce national health schemes and the like—at the price of the occurrence of unpre-dicted and undesired consequences that nullify the benefits supposed to flow from the original "planning". In his early pro-Communist days Anderson, though already aware of "the difficulties of social prediction", was prepared to support large-scale social planning because he took it that Communists would try to implement their plans in a careful, scientific way. "If ", we find him writing, "we have a definite theory of society, we are bound to make predictions, and though these will occasionally be wrong, this will enable us to correct our theory; and we shall, besides, have the whole of past history in which to look for verifications." (*T.C.* December 1927 p. 13) But subsequent his-tory, he found, falsified his expectations, and verified instead "the absurdity of the pretences of the advocates of a 'planned society'". (S p. 335) Such supposed "scientific" planners, when indeed they have any theoretical conception of what they are about, simply fall back on the assumption of overall prediction and overall control, which is not only thoroughly mistaken, but has as its main consequence the unforeseen promotion of forces inimical to human liberty.

Anderson's considered assessment of Marxism thus leads us back to *ethics*. In his judgement there are two rival strains in Marxist thinking, the scientific-objective approach to how that complex phenomenon, society, goes on and the unscientific-salvationist aspiration of "saving" society in the interests of an imagined solidarist ideal, and the opposition between the two reflects a vital distinction of ethical outlooks. "The doctrine of history as struggle is at once the liberal and the scientific part of Marxism; the doctrine of socialism as something to be established ('classless society') is its servile part." (S p. 339) Anderson, of course, discerned comparatively early the authoritarian-servile character of the regime being developed in the U.S.S.R. and this knowledge influences his ethical appraisal of Marxism. He also observes how later aspirant Marxists, "despite Marx's criticism of reformism on this very point", came more and more to resemble reformists in affecting "to stand outside society and adjust it" and to "employ more and more the ideology of philanthropy or betterment" (DI p. 17)—and we can add that, since Anderson's time, the same outlook has, with not many exceptions, been characteristic of both the Old and the New Left. But if what Anderson regards as the "philanthropic-salvationist" approach to social issues was less pronounced among radicals in the nineteenth and early twentieth centuries this is not to say that Marx himself was exempt from it. Anderson argues that the philanthropic-salvationist strain is certainly present in Marx's thinking in the form of his interest in "making history" and in finally overcoming all social antagonisms, and these unscientific ideas exist alongside the other scientific strain in which Marx criticises the Utopian Socialists and thinks of the workers as struggling for liberation by the exercise of their initiative and responsibility. Or, in terms of the distinction made by Sorel, whom Anderson follows here, there is a division within the thought of Marx and some of his followers between the ethic of the consumer and that of the producer, the latter being anti-servile and anti-salvationist and involving the kinds of activities in which, Anderson suggests, Marx himself "recognises positive goodness". (RA p.165)

SOREL AND OTHER SOCIAL THINKERS

Apart from Marx and his followers, Sorel is the social thinker who most influenced Anderson, though he also paid attention, in particular, to the views of Vico, Croce, Bernstein, Nomad and Burnham.

Georges Sorel (1847–1922), who influenced Anderson's ethics, was a French social philosopher who, in his most significant work, is an unusual combination of an unorthodox Marxist and an advocate of syndicalism. But though Sorel was a prodigious writer of books and articles and was in his time very influential, he is nowadays—unlike a number of other past radical theorists —largely unremembered; consequently it may be of value to begin by recalling his work in outline.

There were a number of variations in Sorel's views and sympathies, some of which must have been quite repugnant to Anderson—if, indeed, he had knowledge of these parts of Sorel's work. Thus, in an early book, Sorel actually took the quite un-Andersonian stand of arguing that the Athenians were perfectly justified in condemning Socrates to death, and in some of his initial proletarian writings Sorel upheld the values of working class chastity and family life! However, in his important social studies Sorel was influenced first by Proudhon and then by Marx —so that he became, and in some ways always remained, an interesting kind of "anarcho-Marxist". He also had particular contact with Italian thinkers, exchanging ideas with the Marxist, Labriola, and with Croce, Pareto and Michels. Early in this century, like many other French radicals, Sorel was a defender of Dreyfus in the "Dreyfus Case", but later was repelled by the opportunism and profiteering of left-wing "Dreyfusard" politicians, and went on to write his most famous work, *Reflections on Violence* (first French edition and English translation, 1908) which elaborated and defended anarcho-syndicalism. Later, becoming disillusioned by the working class, and disturbed by the continuing corruption of the politicians, he was for a short time before 1914 in touch with the right-wing *Action Française*, but that ceased when members of that organisation proved themselves to be vociferous patriots on the outbreak of war. Critical of both sides during the war, including both French and German socialist "patriots", Sorel renewed his enthusiasm for the proletariat with the advent of the Bolshevik Revolution and, like various other French syndicalists, dropped his previous objection to *political party* action. He became an admirer of Lenin who, he said, unlike for example Napoleon, does not wish "to create a new aristocracy on the model of the old", and who, Sorel believed, was ushering in a proletarian society in which there was genuine grass-roots participation by the workers in the running of Russian affairs. However, not long before he died Sorel expressed grave doubts about the revolution. Noting the "insufficient maturity" of the Russian workers and the presence of "a large number of corrupt officials" he foresaw the outcome to be the creation of "a new bourgeoisie".[40]

But among Sorel's multifarious writings, it was only *Reflections on Violence*, the short work *La Decomposition du Marxisme*, 1908, and (mainly for its criticism of Christian morality) *La Ruine du Monde Antique*, 1901, that influenced Anderson and helped him to shape his views on ethics and on what is defensible and indefensible in Marxism.

In his treatment of Marxism, Sorel had some affinities with Bernstein who, about the turn of the century, provoked a celebrated controversy among German Marxists and was strongly criticised for his "revisionism" by Kautsky, the "titular" Marxist theorist after the death of Engels. Bernstein had variegated and not altogether clear views, some of which were rejected by Sorel. In particular, he was in effect a reformist, but he did maintain (correctly in the light of its later history) that the German Social Democratic Party was largely hypocritical in its protestations since it was, above all, a parliamentary party with no real concern with bringing about revolution. He further maintained (making a point of particular interest to Anderson) that if the

---

[40] Review of S. Zagorsky, *La République des Soviets*, Paris, Pavot, 1921, *La Revue communiste*, April 1921, p. 135.

workers are to emancipate themselves, they need to develop political maturity by acquiring a training in political and economic organisation within democratic society, class-ridden though it be—rather than, we can say with the advantage of hindsight, having quite immature and inexperienced workers attempting to conduct affairs after a sudden revolution. Where, in particular, there is an affinity between Sorel and Bernstein —and an influence on Anderson—is in their view of the Marxist legacy. Sorel, maintaining as he does that Marx and Engels, hindered by polemics, never gave a clear exposition of historical materialism, agrees with Bernstein, as against Kautsky, that there are antagonistic elements in Marxism, namely a concern with emancipation on the part of the worker-producers themselves as against concern with political action aiming at control of society. In line with this, Sorel, like Anderson, applauds Bernstein's observation that "the end is nothing, the movement is everything".

Sorel's own position, developed in *Reflections on Violence* is that the redemption of society—from the corruption of business and politics and in general the servile and self-interested outlook manifested in "the ethic of the consumer"—can only be achieved through the co-operative activity of the workers. Though Sorel does indeed uphold violence, particularly the use of the general strike, he does not really look to some final solution in a utopian future, for even the general strike is in the main a "myth", an ideal to motivate the workers. He looks instead to constant struggle and enterprising, self-help activities here and now on the part of the workers, the producers of society. Such workers, he says, are "men who do participate in the real working-class movement", they shun politicians including "the dignitaries of Parliamentary Socialism", they are not actuated by "a *morality of the weak*", but seek "to *create today the ethic of the producers of the future*".

Sorel, who was also influenced in part by Nietzsche, finds further illustrations of the producer's ethic in past history. To cite two of his examples, one concerns "the free men" of the French revolutionary armies in 1792–94 whom he contrasts with the "automatons" both of the royal armies and of Napoleon's later armies. "Battles under these conditions could," he writes, "no longer be likened to games of chess in which each man is comparable to a pawn; they become collections of heroic exploits accomplished by individuals under the influence of an extraordinary enthusiasm." So much so, Sorel further comments, we might "be led to ask if our official Socialists, with their passion for discipline, and their infinite confidence in the genius of their leaders, are not the authentic inheritors of the traditions of the royal armies, while the anarchists and the upholders of the general strike represent at the present time the spirit of the revolutionary warriors". The second example concerns the anonymous "great Gothic artists" who, in the erection and sculpturing of medieval cathedrals, without seeking personal rewards or personal fame, nevertheless produced masterpieces. It is values of these kinds, Sorel argues, that characterise the emancipated enterprising worker—in contrast with the state of mind of "the working classes who have been educated by politicians; all they are fit for is to change their masters".

The attractiveness to Anderson of this kind of Sorelian morality of commitment, co-operation and initiative vis-à-vis being acquisitive, servile and reliant on "superiors", will be evident and such a conception, as will be amplified in Part II is at the heart of Anderson's view of the nature of political freedom and democracy. But he follows Sorel in agreeing with the values he espouses, rather than with his belief that the modern working class is the embodiment of those values because, while Anderson shared that belief for a time, it is not part of his definitive position—and, incidentally, even when he held it, he stressed the idea of co-operation between workers' movements and *intellectual* ones. Thus, while he grants that early in the century many workers may perhaps have exhibited the ethic of the producer, his mature judgement is that nowadays "proletarians ... in spite of Sorel, do not exhibit the producer's mentality (the condition of co-operation) but are concerned with being better off, with reform". (S p. 186)

In Anderson's view, then, the kind of ethico-political activities that he and Sorel commend—along with Marx some of the time —are not carried on by the workers, in particular, or any other large segment of society; they are essentially kept alive by various minority forces that have to struggle constantly for their existence. In consequence, he is also receptive to the ideas of a number of other thinkers who question, in a pessimistic but realistically pluralist way, the "salvationist" belief in the final coming of social progress and harmony.

Therefore, like various other social philosophers, Anderson finds merit in Vico's view of social struggles, both because of his anticipation of Marx and because, in contrast with the latter's conception of an ultimate "classless society", Vico takes it that social struggles will never cease. Likewise, Anderson thinks highly of the more ethical conception of the permanence of struggle that is found in Croce's view of the varying fortunes of *liberty* as it declines and then is reborn in conditions of adversity. "On this view", as Anderson puts it, "both liberty and servility are features of society at any stage." (S p. 335) He is, however, critical of Croce on some other counts, including one of misunderstanding Marx. Thus Croce claims that Marx subordinates all values to "his one ruling interest, economic welfare and the social revolution", but this, Anderson observes in an interesting comment, "is an obviously biased judgement, since, whatever the defects of Marx's view of production, it is not a doctrine of 'welfare' in the sense of personal comfort".[41]

In view of Anderson's firm commitment to political autonomy and initiative and his corresponding opposition to the exercise of servility-inducing State power, it may be asked, what is his view of *anarchism*? The somewhat surprising answer is that he makes few references to the subject but, as may be judged from his use of the term "anarchy" in the sense of "chaos" or "absence of co-operation" (for example, *T.C.* December 1927 p. 13; EP p. 25), his attitude, at any rate to classical anarchism, is an antipathetic one. This appears to be because he dismisses anarchists as utopian thinkers whose one merit, a concern with bringing moral questions into social theory, is marred by their atomism and voluntarism. This criticism, we may observe, while it may well apply to many anarchists and especially "individualist anarchists", is hardly fair at least to Bakunin, who to a large extent accepted Marx's historical materialism and theory of the class struggle. However, as against that, we can note the following: Anderson does at one point complain about Marx's "misrepresentation of Proudhon" on economics (*A.H.* 1938 p. 16); there is the fact of Anderson's apparent approval of Sorel's anarchist tendencies; and, in addition, his sympathy for the view of Max Nomad, a writer describable in some ways as a "pessimistic anarchist".[42] Nomad takes the position that all revolutions are "betrayed" and that twentieth century revolutions profit, not the masses in whose name they are carried out, but the new politicians and office-holders who come to power in the wake of the revolution; consequently, he holds, freedom lies in

[41] Review of B. Croce, *My Philosophy and other Essays on the Moral and Political Problems of Our Time*, London, Allen and Unwin, 1949. *A.J.P.*, December 1959, p. 259.
[42] Anderson was receptive to Nomad's writings in *The Modern Monthly* in the mid 1930s, and, for example, referred approvingly to his view in a course of lectures he gave in 1947 on "Marx and Modern Thought".

"perpetual opposition", that is, in a permanent, unending struggle for emancipation by the "underdog" both against his "old masters" and against the "new masters" who take over from them.

Another writer with some influence on Anderson is James Burnham who, in *The Managerial Revolution*, puts forward a view similar to Nomad's—though unlike Nomad, he places no stress on *opposing* the forces concerned. According to Burnham, capitalism is indeed declining as Marx predicted, but is being replaced by a new type of totalitarian regime—which may indifferently be Communist or Fascist—in which power passes to a new class of rulers, especially economic managers, who owe their position to their control of the State apparatus. Anderson largely endorses this view, which of course fits in with his criticisms of the Marxist theory of the State, and he connects it, in particular, with his own conception of the "servile State". By this he understands the modern trend, in "democratic" as well as other countries, towards State regimentation and control under the guise of promoting the solidarist—and servile—ideals of "welfare" and "security"; and these ideals ironically (he argues as we have seen) are wrongly supposed to be achieved by "scientific planning". He disagrees, however, with Burnham's emphasis on the *managers* as the leading members of the new ruling class and maintains that "This involves an underestimation of *political* monopoly, of the importance of centralised direction by 'the party'." (S p. 333) Moreover, as we should expect, Anderson finds it a weakness of Burnham's position that he ignores *moral* issues and tries to leave out altogether, for example, questions about the enterprising, or the servile, character of the differing social forces he is discussing.

THEORY OF DEMOCRACY AND EDUCATION

As is disclosed to some extent in the discussion in the previous chapter of Marx and of Sorel, a vital ingredient in Anderson's overall position is his view of *democracy*, with which is linked in certain ways his also vital view of *education*. In the case of his treatment of these two subjects there is a particular interweaving of questions of theory with ones about policy, for, as well as advancing his conception of what, objectively, genuine democracy and genuine education consist in, he is also deeply concerned to defend or promote them vis-à-vis social forces inimical to their well-being. It is, however, possible to disentangle the two approaches in his writings and I will here sum up his theoretical approach, leaving his policies for more explicit mention in Part II.

Democracy

Since the word "democracy" and its cognates are eulogistic, emotionally-laden and indeed, ideological terms it is not surprising that their use commonly covers up divergent interpretations of just what democracy is. Anderson, however, points out that this is a feature of most widely used political terms and should not deter us from seeking to find positive content in the notion of democracy. Thus, even though the standard or prevailing conception of Western democracy is one of "representative government" by means of universal suffrage, scrutiny reveals that the social process involved is not really a democratic one because there is no question of, for instance, Australia being a community in which a large majority of citizens play a significant part in making decisions about business that affects the community as a whole. An example Anderson cites more than once is the case of foreign affairs where very little knowledge, let alone decision-making, is vouchsafed to anyone but a tiny minority of leading politicians and public servants. Representation, he argues, whether or not it is necessary, is certainly not sufficient for democracy. Thus the average citizen, who is propagandised by media organs over which he has no control, is largely uninformed about political issues and he is not encouraged by governments and other entrenched forces to think critically about those issues; as an elector he is merely confronted by a choice between two main parties whose policies he has not helped to formulate and of which he has no clear understanding, and once he has exercised his "democratic" right to vote, responsibility is left entirely in the hands of the politicians for whom he has voted. As Anderson puts it in one succinct formulation, the ordinary political process deprives people "of *active* citizenship and degrades them to the level of *passive* citizenship; it makes politics a matter for governments, and citizens mere voting machines". (*W.W.* 8 November 1929)

So a positive requirement of democracy is active citizenship, the possession by large numbers of the people of political understanding and the exercise by them of political initiative and responsibility. However, that is not the sole requirement —or at least it has to be enlarged on to avoid erroneous interpretations. Thus, if we express ourselves merely in terms of the average citizen or voter we may be construed as endorsing social atomism, as believing—like many political utopians—that to fulfil the "democratic ideal" we merely need more and more individuals who, *qua* individuals, cast their votes in an aware, rational way. But that, in Anderson's view, is an inadequate account of democracy; we have to pay careful attention to the more important part played by social organisations and movements. Thus, even though we may often—as for example in Australia—safely judge that most citizens are passive, politically uneducated voters, it does not follow that there is not some measure of democracy and political freedom. For, despite the abrogation, in the electoral process, of political responsibility to politicians and bureaucratic functionaries, there is still an interplay of social forces through which interests can be asserted and rights fought for. It is recognition of this that led Anderson to maintain, even in his pro-Communist days—and contrary, for example to Lenin—that the workers exercise some democratic weight in Western capitalist societies, as is illustrated by the following passage:

> It is incorrect to say that the workers have no rights under capitalism, for that would be to say that they have no power. Rights are simply claims backed by force—demands that can be made good. And the workers have made good their right to be politically active; they have carried on organisation and agitation; they have formed unions and parties; conducted industrial struggles and political campaigns. This is the measure of their enfranchisement; their economic and political achievements, and not the "right" to individual employment or to an individual vote, constitute the existing rights, the actual power, of the working class. (FC p. 7)

Here Anderson takes a more sympathetic and a more monolithic view of the working class than he does in his later thought, but his comments make evident what conception of political freedom he is advancing and how it can be applied to the exercise of social strength by other groups and organisations.

There is, therefore, a close connection between Anderson's view of democracy and his social pluralism. The latter, as we have seen, is a *category* of social science, that is, all societies are pluralist owing to the presence in all of them of a diversity of social forces, but there can be important variations in the strength and character, including the moral character, of these forces, and it is these variations that enable us to class particular societies as markedly democratic, markedly undemocratic, democratic to some extent, and so on. As flows from Anderson's views on the "servile State", a fundamental condition of the presence of democracy in a community is the existence of a variety of organisations, and the like, which, though they do in part conflict with one another and themselves contain conflicting tendencies, have considerable independent strength. Contrary to solidarist conceptions of democracy, "independent activity, involving, at times, opposition to the State, is not opposed to democracy; it is essential to it". (PD p. 9) That is why he places so much stress on the exercise of rights of opposition, including the right to strike, which is a formidable check on the power of the State, and also the right to enjoy freedom of public discussion, because democracy, he holds, resides "in the openness, the publicity, of struggle". (*A.J.P.P.* 1943 p. 56) He also characteristically observes that the practice of democracy involves, not an illogical meeting of tyranny with tyranny, but dealing in a *democratic* way with undemocratic views and interests.

At the same time, as well as questions about opposition to the State, there is the further significant question of the degree to which the various social organisations, in the conduct of their affairs, are themselves marked by rank and file participation as against direction from above; informed, open discussion as against secrecy; recognition as against suppression of minority interests; and so on. We can ask which of these conditions obtain in the case of the State apparatus as well as in the case of other organisations, but in Anderson's view the State as an organisation, being so conspicuously bureaucratic-hierarchical in its way of working, is unlikely in any instance ever to be more than marginally democratic. The history of organisations in these regards discloses a wide variety of cases. Thus, a trade union or a political party may assist democracy by being a force that to some extent counterbalances the State, but when we examine how their own transactions are decided and carried out, we find (in practice as distinct from professed ideology) that some unions and parties are, and some are not, relatively democratic organisations. Or, in the disparate cases, say of a religious organisation fighting against persecution, or a newspaper corporation that exposes the errors or pretensions of a government, we may have some degree of internal democracy, but much more commonly, of course, such bodies are run in a thoroughly authoritarian and hierarchical manner. Or, again, to cite a specific, more unusual example, consider, in the case of the Boer War, the fact that the army on the Boer side appears to have had a remarkably democratic form of organisation and yet existed alongside State and Church institutions that were quite undemocratic.

To sum up, in Anderson's view, the measure of democracy in a society depends (1) on the amount of strength other organisations have vis-à-vis the State; (2) the extent to which, in the consideration of and, for example, voting on, general community affairs, there is informed participation by the mass of the population; and (3) the extent to which the State and more especially other important social organisations have internal ways of working that are democratic in character.

Education

"The unexamined life is not worth living", Anderson quotes Socrates with approval (S p. 206), and that Socratic conception of education, as something general that combines or co-ordinates the development of the spirit of criticism with the living of a worthwhile way of life, is at the heart of Anderson's own view. "A liberal education", he writes, "is one which enables us to live *freely*. It is a training, not for a particular job or service, but for a whole life." (EP p. 55) Consequently, he regards the subordination of learning and criticism to utilitarian and commercial considerations as being utterly opposed to education. The pupil, from the earliest stages, needs to be taught to think for himself to the extent that is consonant with his powers, and that is something that can be best achieved by adopting a broad approach. "All the subjects studied", he argues, "should be brought into the closest connection, . . . classics, literature, history and science should be taught as parts of a single culture (and this, it may be noted, implies that the specialist 'subject teacher' should, as far as possible, give place to the class teacher)." (EP p. 60)

A broad approach also enables the pupil to begin to question received opinions and traditions including, not least, those promulgated by the State—for Anderson, of course, criticises the passive, anti-democratic notions of preparation for "citizenship" or "service to the community" that are so often extolled by custodians of the young. In his view, education includes *political* education and so requires treatment of pupils as responsible beings and not as servile objects of indoctrination. Naturally, he draws no distinction in this regard between the sexes, and incidentally argues that "absence of co-education in the schools leads to the inclusion of women among the lower orders". (EP p. 57) Similarly, in the case of teachers, as against the servile status that they are supposed to have in relation to their masters or employers, such as the Department of Education, he argues for the treatment of teachers as free men who are entitled to autonomy and to the right to express opinions and criticisms about the institutions in which they work. Likewise, he takes it to be educationally important for both pupils and teachers that "controversial" subjects such as history and social science—and religion to the minimal extent it is suitable as a school subject at all—should not be dealt with dogmatically, but in a controversial, that is a critical and pluralist, way.

In opposing prevalent utilitarian and social service conceptions of education, Anderson draws attention to their solidarist assumption—usually in a concealed or implicit way—of social unity, and against this he advances his two standard criticisms: (1) The proponents of that view are open to the difficulty Marx indicated when he asked: "Who will educate the educators?";

that is, they naively assume that they are "above" society and do not see that, in fact, they represent *particular* social interests as against others; and (2), partly as a consequence of (1), their practical "plans" are far from being scientific or efficient, but are marked by improvisation and hoping for the best. So, far from finding that the "new education" is promoting the total interest of society, we are once more led—in line, for example, with Nomad and Burnham—to the view that in so far as any clearly articulated interests are being promoted, they are the interests of governmental and educational *careerists*. Or, in politico-democratic terms, we have one more instance of the continuing struggle between liberality and illiberality, in this case between the cause of critical inquiry and that of State organised "social utility".

Anderson makes parallel observations about university education, a branch of the subject on which he naturally concentrates in his writings. In line with his views on school education, what he takes to be the core of university education—and what he vigorously advocates—is a broad, liberal, *classical* approach. He expresses antipathy to the narrow classicism that has so often been associated with Oxford and Cambridge and the training of a ruling political elite, but, understanding the subject to be freed from the pedantry in which it sometimes flounders, he takes the study of classics, especially Greek philosophy, history and literature, as no mere antiquarian pursuit, but an intellectual activity that can help the student to come to grips with quite contemporary problems. More widely, he understands the classical approach to involve an attachment to liberal education and to an *objective* outlook. "Classicism", he says, "stands for the unity of culture against all forms of subjectivism and interestedness." (S p. 202) Of course, among the tendencies that pervade universities not only are there various powerful anti-educational interests, such as administrative ones, but also, he holds, in areas closer to thought and investigation there are problems created by the conflicts between the classical-critical outlook he admires and the constantly burgeoning scientific-practicalist approach. His position, however, is not classicist or traditionalist in the sense of being opposed to *science*; indeed he deplores any sharp separation of science from the other elements of culture; but he does criticise the narrow utilitarian conception of science, which, he argues, involves a false view of scientific inquiry and has played into the hands of the planners and practicalists, and contributed to the general decline of learning and literacy. In consequence, he stresses the place of faculties of Arts in universities, holding that despite the tendency Arts subjects have towards narrow specialisation, those faculties are virtually alone in keeping alive a broad approach to culture and criticism. For like reasons he applauds, as an essential part of university life, participation by students in such extra-curricular matters as the activities of intellectual and political societies and the writing of material for student publications.

As an upholder of educational values, it is Anderson's view that the running of universities is properly the province of the people who work and study in them, and not of councils etc., that consist largely of the representatives of outside business and governmental interests. But he recognised, of course, that that was a forlorn utopian hope, even in the days before there was substantial State intervention in university affairs. On the latter issue, however, we find him arguing, with early foresight, that the cause of genuine university education would be best furthered if universities could stand firm and, instead of yielding to utilitarian pressures and the blandishments of large-scale State aid, remain *small* but *independent* institutions (and thus, incidentally, strengthen democratic pluralism). For otherwise, so runs a prophecy he made more than three decades ago, if universities "adopt the criterion of social usefulness (in the place of their own criterion of scholarship) they will soon be technical institutions". (*A.J.P.P.* 1943 p. 62)

It is thus evident how Anderson's conceptions of education as critical thinking and democracy as active, aware citizenship coalesce. "Neither democracy nor education", he insists, "can exist without controversy, they cannot exist without initiative, without spontaneous movements of the 'rank and file', and the greatest danger to both is the spurious agreement involved in submission to the 'expert'." (*A.J.P.P.* 1943 p. 60) Democracy and education, in his view, are jointly involved in the permanent struggle against forces conducive to political and intellectual regimentation and as such are very important manifestations of *good* activities, or, as he also maintains, following Croce, of the activities that make history "the story of liberty".

PART II: POLITICAL HISTORY AND PUBLIC CONTROVERSIES

COMMUNISM; FREETHOUGHT
CONTROVERSIES, 1927–1932

Anderson, then aged thirty-three, arrived in Sydney on 10 March 1927 to take up the post of Challis Professor in the University of Sydney and, as he returned abroad only once, in 1938, he spent the mature, second half of his life almost entirely in Sydney. It was here, moreover, that he did much of his thinking, and all his writing, about social and ethical questions. He had in his native Scotland been an early sympathiser with Socialism along with his father Alexander, a country headmaster, and his elder brother William, another philosopher. For, in company with them, he had, while a student at Glasgow University, been involved in speaking and working on behalf of the Socialist cause—though in line with his later characteristic thought, they were all concerned with bringing education, including political education, to the workers, rather than with electing politicians to represent them in parliament.[43] But then after becoming a lecturer in Philosophy, briefly in the Universities of Cardiff and Glasgow and from 1920 to 1926 in the University of Edinburgh, he was absorbed by philosophy and paid comparatively little attention to social and political matters. Then, in 1926, the British general strike occurred, a very significant political event in which rank and file unionists were impressively resolute and self-reliant, despite vilification of them by establishment forces and the weak approach of the Labour Party and the Trade Union Council

---

[43] It is worth remarking also that prior to 1920 William Anderson (who was Professor of Philosophy in Auckland University College from 1921 to 1955) wrote various articles for *The New Age* that were sympathetic to "Guild Socialism", a position which, in respect of its opposition to State control and centralised administration, has affinities with John Anderson's views on democratic pluralism.

leaders who ultimately capitulated to the employers. Anderson, dismayed by this course of events, began to have contact with Communists in Edinburgh and to study Marxist and Communist literature. Thus it was that, while much of his general philosophy and also his literary theory had been worked out to a considerable extent before he came to Australia, it was virtually only when he arrived here that he was beginning to think hard about issues of social philosophy.

The C.P.A.

Sydney in 1927, as now, was the headquarters of the Communist Party of Australia, and Anderson soon became associated with local Communists who at one stage gave him the title of "Theoretical Adviser" of the Party, even though he never became a member of it. In the next five years, but mostly in 1927–1929, he made various contributions (in all fourteen) to the Australian Communist publications, bringing to them a freshness of approach and a level of argument not previously—or afterwards—found in them. It is worth noting, however, as something that was no doubt attractive to Anderson, that local Communists—differing from their approach in the 1930s—were not then averse to genuine and theoretical discussion and the Party leaders of that period, J. Kavanagh and his opponent, H.J. Moxon, who succeeded him, both reveal in their writings powers of discussion that plainly excel the efforts of the subsequent leaders, J.B. Miles and L. Sharkey.

Anderson's first Communist article, on the subject of "Art and the Workers" (*W.W.* 19 June 1927), criticised the "artistic leftism" of a previous writer who maintained that the workers should shun bourgeois music and that all art is corrupt which is "born of corrupt environment". According to this view, Anderson pointed out, the character of a production is supposed to be determined by the epoch in which it was produced, so that Lenin's books, written during the epoch of imperialism, ought themselves to count as being imperialistic—when in fact, as against this, the starting point of proletarian thinking has to be found in bourgeois thought as is evidenced by the way in which Marx and Lenin rightly utilised the work of bourgeois writers. We must not, then, Anderson argued, in the case of literature, fall into the error of believing that a writer like Jack London (who really propagates bourgeois exploitative ideas) is a "revolutionary" merely because he writes about strikes or revolts, or that, for example, Meredith cannot expose bourgeois illusions because his novels are concerned with bourgeois people. Likewise, with music, "If the workers do not learn from the best bourgeois music, they will absorb the worst, and we shall have to think of them marching joyfully to victory to strains as pointless and dreary as that of 'The Red Flag'." Janet Anderson it may be observed, subsequently advanced a similar position when, writing under her maiden name of Janet C. Baillie, she criticised a facile view that had been put forward to the effect that Shakespeare could be dismissed because his characters were principally upper class ones.[44]

Anderson next turned to the question of revolution and, in an article entitled "Evolution and Revolution" (*W.W.* 15 July 1927) he sharply criticised reformism or gradualism, thus taking up a standpoint he was to adhere to throughout the various phases in his thought and which was, moreover, a topical one in that the recurrent question of whether or not to support the reformist Australian Labour Party grew into a fundamental dispute among Communists in 1929. The following extract from the opening part of the article will indicate the style and temper of his argument:

> The discussion of gradualism in recent issues emphasises the necessity, in present day controversy, of making the term "evolution" clear. Reformists use the assertion that society evolves as a reason for rejecting revolution altogether. On the other hand, we have the opportunist view that, for the most part, social conditions develop of their own accord, but that at certain unspecified, or vaguely specified, times revolutionary action is both opportune and necessary.
>
> But, as a matter of fact, there is no real contrast between evolution and revolution. On the contrary, the revolutionist is precisely the person who correctly applies evolutionary conceptions to society, while the reformist thinks of society as constructively created by pure reason. . . .

Evolution, he went on to argue, is a form of revolutionary transformation, for it proceeds by continual struggle for existence in which certain species, or certain varieties within a species, establish themselves and others are defeated and destroyed. The social parallel of this, in Communist terms, is that there is a struggle for

---

[44] "Shakespeare and the Workers, A Reply to V.F. Calverton", *The Communist*, 1 February 1928, pp. 26–32.

existence between capitalistic and proletarian forms of organisation, but while the former have hitherto been dominant, an important variation in capitalism is occurring. This is its becoming imperialist and financially exploitative—Anderson here was advancing Lenin's view—which has strengthened workers' organisations, enabling them to become dominant in Russia, and favouring them in a worldwide struggle for revolutionary power.

A little later Anderson took the most unusual course for a professor at Sydney University of writing a letter to *The Sydney Morning Herald* in which he *criticised* that newspaper's stand on the Sacco and Vanzetti Case. When these two American immigrants, who were widely believed to have been victims of a "frame-up" for murder because of their anarchist opinions, were finally executed in Boston in August 1927, there were worldwide protests and demonstrations and radicals generally were deeply disturbed by the event. The American writer, John dos Passos, captured the anguish and anger of himself and other protesters on the spot when he made the attempt to save Sacco and Vanzetti the climax of his powerful work *U.S.A.*—compare the memorable "Camera Eye" (No. 50): "they have clubbed us off the streets, they are stronger, they are rich . . .". But in Australia *The Sydney Morning Herald* was unimpressed by the campaign on behalf of Sacco and Vanzetti and when they were executed, came out with an editorial, headed "Sheep!", attacking the protest demonstration held in Sydney. Anderson, in a carefully reasoned letter, criticised the *Herald* view, pointing out that:

> What has been most specifically alleged by the defenders of Sacco and Vanzetti is that the case was deliberately "framed up" by the police of Massachusetts, and that the police were aided and abetted by the judiciary of that State in bringing to the electric chair two men whose real offence was that of being political agitators. . . . Responsible members of the United States Government have stated that Sacco and Vanzetti were dangerous to the State, and have advanced this as an additional reason for putting them to death, though it was not in the least what they were tried for. Again, much emphasis has been placed on the fact that the two men were atheists. . . . (*S.M.H.* 25 August 1927)

In a later editorial (1 September) the *Herald* made the remarkable statement that "had the solicitude for Sacco and Vanzetti been genuine, the protests would have ceased with their death", but in writing a further critical letter Anderson was to learn that quality of argument was not enough to secure a hearing by the

Press, for the *Herald* published neither this letter nor another one he wrote soon afterwards criticising a *Herald* editorial on Communism. In subsequent years daily newspapers would not publish a letter by him (in 1930) protesting against a refusal by the Town Hall authorities to allow Communists to speak there and another one (in 1932) on the dangers to political liberty of the New Guard. (These letters were published in *The Workers' Weekly*.)

Anderson next advanced the first of his many criticisms of censorship when, under the heading "Politics and Publicity, Are We to be Allowed to Discuss Communism?" (*W.W.* 14 October 1927) he objected to the extraordinary Australian censorship of that time which declared to be prohibited imports *The Communist Manifesto* of Marx and Engels and forty-one other works by Lenin, Trotsky, Stalin and other Communists. Reanimadverting on *The Sydney Morning Herald*, Anderson referred to one of its editorial pronouncements that in any country under the British flag, "the freedom of a man's mind to think and read and believe what he likes is absolute" and pointed out the inconsistency between this claim and the prevailing censorship which, in the absence of Australian books on Communism, allowed the condemnation of that position, as in the daily Press, to go practically unchallenged. As against that state of affairs he put the case for political education, based on full and free discussion, in a way which is still very apt, whether the topic remains Communism or we substitute other topics for it. Any voter, he wrote, for example, who has not read some Communist books "is condemning himself as unfit to vote either for or against Communism. In short, are we, Communists and non-Communists alike, to be allowed to discuss Communism? Or are we to regard ourselves as political infants, and to assume (1) that public opinion consists of the opinions of newspaper proprietors, (2) that political discussion is politically dangerous, (3) that the only thing that prevents us all from becoming Communists is our ignorance of what Communism is? Surely not."

In 1927–1928 there was a brief revival of *The Communist*, theoretical organ of the Communist Party which had run from 1924 to 1926. Anderson wrote for it three articles which, together with two articles he later wrote for the Melbourne University *Proletariat*, set out his position as a pro-Communist. In his articles for *The Communist*[45] he was specifically concerned to attack reformism, defend revolution and to stress what he called "the

---

[45] These articles and some of his contributions to *The Workers' Weekly* were written under the name of "A. Spencer". One conjecture is that this pseudonym was humorously derived by Anderson from the name of the English chain stores, "Marks and Spencer".

moral factor in the revolution". Criticising on the one hand the bourgeois believer in the merits of today's supposed orderly society and on the other hand, the utopian believer in peaceful progress through the exercise of human goodwill, Anderson argued that neither has "even begun to consider what society really is". But the Communist, in line with the Marxist view that it is not merely a matter of explaining society but one of trans-forming it, accepts the fact of capitalist disorder and social unrest and, instead of standing still and "impartially" watching society as if he were not part of it, makes use of his knowledge of social theory to predict developments and, in the light of these predic-tions, intervenes in society in an effort to bring about a mature, non-capitalist society. Now there are limits to social prediction so that occasional mistakes will have to be corrected as he goes along, but the Communist is drawing on a knowledge of history, in particular about the progressive place in it of the working class. Thus, its "power of co-operation, evolved as a defence against oppression, is what entitles the working class to be re-garded as the society of the future. It is in this sense that history is on their side." (*T.C.* December 1927 p. 14) The argument for revolution and the chances for its success, Anderson insisted, were very much dependent on the moral character of the working class. In the Marxist view, capitalism prepares the way for revolution and the proletariat carries it out, but it is a mistake to think, as Marxists commonly do, that the incentive to revolu-tion is merely an economic interest in a greater return for labour and that it does not *also* involve a moral interest in a way of living which is "broadly describable as freedom".

> Granted that it is among the oppressed working class that revolutionism does take hold, it would be meaningless with-out some conception of a better society for which capitalist society has prepared the way but to which it is at present a hindrance. Thus a recognition of the positive evils of present day society, and of the positive goods which the rising proletariat is to secure, is an essential part of revolu-tionism. (*T.C.* February 1928 p. 8)

The proletariat, moreover, in advancing the cause of a better society, does so as an aware mass-acting *class*, and that is why humanitarian and reformist views, setting out vague programmes based on the altruism of individuals and eschewing violence, must be rejected. "Denying in effect the very existence of the class struggle, the reformists appear as the most thorough-going defenders of the established order." (*T.C.* June 1928 p. 15) Even the capitalists, he held, sometimes recognise classes, as when they resort to class action on behalf of their own class, but the reformists repudiate class conflict altogether, by condemning violence when it comes from the masses and by apparently believing that "the pure principles of individual justice are observed in such acts as the execution of Sacco and Vanzetti, and the shooting of Chinese trade unionists". (ibid.)

Anderson thus accepted at this time Marx's theory of the class struggle, Lenin's additions to it concerning imperialism, the Communist view that the Russian Revolution had ushered in a genuine workers' society, and that similar revolutions, as distinct from mere reformist measures, were necessary in other countries, including Australia. In accepting Marx's historical materialism, however, he at no time gave credence to the vagaries of the "dialectic" and he was, furthermore, critical of the simple view of some Communists that it was just a matter of "hating the bosses" and of advancing the workers' economic interests, these often being understood in the narrowest material benefits sense. In other words, he rejected what is sometimes called "Vulgar Marxism"[46] in favour of a more complex view and, in particular, saw the role of the working class as that of a revolutionary social and moral force whose enterprising, co-operative way of living would lead to an overall regeneration of society.

Anderson, moreover, had his own distinctive way of formulating and reasoning on the issues and, as against the loose and emotional thinking often found in Communist circles, he held that "on any question, vital or not vital, which the Party deals with, it is vital that its position should be stated plainly and unequivocally". (*W.W.* 21 September 1928) An illustration of this view is a criticism he made of the Communist Party when, in a referendum on Prohibition held in New South Wales in September 1928, it urged the workers to vote for Prohibition. Contrary to this, Anderson argued that the militant worker would oppose Prohibition while making it clear what the alignments of

---

[46] Compare, for example, Wilhelm Reich's criticisms of this view, as held by German Communists, in his *Mass Psychology of Fascism*, New York, Farrar, Straus and Giroux, 1970. It is interesting to note that Reich and Anderson each sought to place emphasis on a new factor they thought was consistent with Marx's theory—Reich on a psycho-sexual factor and Anderson, following Sorel, on the moral strength and dedication of the working class—and, further, that each of them in the same period, 1929–1932, Reich in Berlin and Anderson in Sydney, were led, through their opposition to reformism, to support the Comintern line of that time. Compare S. Cooper, "When Reich and Anderson Were Good Stalinists", Sydney Libertarian *Broadsheet*, No. 69, July 1972.

concerned social forces are in this issue. Thus the liquor issue is not an immediately revolutionary one and so there are bourgeois forces on both sides; but the fact that the liquor interests are, of course, concerned only with profiteering at the expense of the workers should not lead the latter to side with the forces seeking Prohibition. For one thing, that question is a "red herring", support for which is a reformist drawing of attention away from revolution and the class struggle; for another thing, he continued, revealing in those early days an incipient distrust of what he later called "the servile State", the movement supporting Prohibition "undoubtedly belongs to the movement for regimentation, for vexatious interference in all the details of life, for the erecting of State force into an unquestioningly accepted standard; in short, for a more and more open dictatorship". Also, even then, he was noticing that Communist leaders were not exempt from criticism, and ended his argument with these words:

> Finally, even to revolutionaries, it may be said: "Be not righteous overmuch." It is easy to say that the Communist Party does not tolerate drunkenness or any other form of inefficiency in its ranks. However, it is possible to be drunk on other things than alcohol—on words, for example, or even on "efficiency". Let it be recognised that the masses will have their diversions, and that interference with these diversions will always be one of the ways in which capitalism makes itself irksome. Whatever be the minor and major issues, the struggle is as broad as society itself, and if party activity is the apex of the revolutionary movement, workers' life is its basis. ("Prohibition", *W.W.* 7 September 1928)

The Commonwealth elections of October 1929 were won by the Labour Party led by Scullin, and the resulting formation of the first Federal Labour Government since 1916 soon brought to a head simmering disquiet and dissension about Labour within Communist ranks. Anderson himself, on the question of censorship, was quick to criticise the new Government for its expressed intention to continue, except for marginal alterations, the existing censorship, and went on to sum up his views in an interesting passage which shows that at all times, including the period when he was sympathetic to the Communist Party, he was a firm advocate of participatory democracy:

> The main point for Australians is that the very existence of such a censorship, and even a *sincere* attempt to define and

exclude the "seditious" leaves the Government with arbitrary powers and interferes with the political rights of individuals and organisations. . . . It is for the Labour Government to make good its democratic pretensions by affirming the right of all citizens to act and think politically all the time, and consequently by allowing them access to all the political material that can be made available. (*W.W.* 8 November 1929)

But the crucial issue for Communists was whether or not they should give political support to the Labour Party and this, before the end of the year, developed into a full-scale conflict—and was one in which Anderson, with his opposition to reformism and his preparedness to criticise the Communist leadership, had a ready-made position. In the past, Australian Communists had oscillated in their attitude to the Labour Party, particularly after they failed, in 1924, to have that Party accept Communists as members of it, though they did tend to support Labour in the ambiguous way advocated by Lenin when he said, for example, with reference to the 1920 British Labour Party leader, "I want with my vote to support Henderson in the same way as the rope supports a hanged man."[47] Thus, in its 1929 Federal election manifesto, the Communist Party said that the Australian Labour Party was a reformist, not a workers', party and was concerned to uphold the interests of the small capitalists and the White Australia Policy; nevertheless the Communist Party, instead of taking up one of the options of having its own candidates stand (as it had done in the N.S.W. elections of 1925) or of advocating an informal vote (the policy pursued in the N.S.W. elections of 1927), urged workers to vote for Labour. In consequence, an attack was mounted on the existing Communist leadership, headed by Jack Kavanagh, who had come to Australia in 1925 after a long record of radicalism in Canada, including being first Chairman of its Communist Party.[48] In particular an attack was made in a long article in *The Workers' Weekly*, signed jointly by H.J. Moxon and L.L. Sharkey, and in a separate criticism by J.B. Miles. Moxon and Sharkey, who claimed that they had been the only opponents of the Central Committee's election policy, referred to Communist opposition to reformism, to the overcoming of the "right-wing"

[47] V.I. Lenin, "*Left-Wing" Communism, An Infantile Disorder, Selected Works*, Vol. 3, Moscow, Progress Publishers, 1975, p. 346.
[48] Compare *The Militant*, March 1940, p. 3.

leadership in parties abroad, and argued that "The political line of the Party must be brought into line with that of the Comintern. Our support of the reformists must cease and as the independent leader of the workers we must win the confidence of that class." (*W.W.* 25 October 1929) At the same time, the Party newspaper threw its pages open to "full and free discussion" and for the next two months there was a remarkable give and take of arguments by Communists on opposing sides.

Anderson's contribution to the discussion had been written as soon as the Party's election manifesto appeared, but was held over for some weeks. He once more criticised the Party's attitude for being too simple, as exemplified in its over-emphasis on "'economic' struggles in the narrowest sense". "The workers' real enemy", he argued, "is not 'the employers', but imperialism. And imperialism is a two-handed fighter. It needs, and gets, the services at one time of Nationalism and at another of 'Labour', it requires to supplement force by fraud." Thus British imperialism had, at that time, two main enemies, American imperialism and Workers' Russia and there was a real danger (which Anderson was then not alone in fearing) of a military strike by Britain at Russia from India, so it was most important to alert the workers to be critical of Labour, for the Australian Labour Government, no less than its British counterpart, would be "an agent of British imperialism, standing for the defeat of the militant workers, for compromise with America and for war with Russia". (*W.W.* 1 November 1929)

In one of his replies to critics, Kavanagh curiously attributed to Anderson the error of "abstraction", that is, of denying that there were oppressive human capitalists when he spoke about imperial*ism* (in the abstract) as the real enemy. But Kavanagh did also argue that in countries like Australia the interests of local capital were now opposed to imperialist capital, and that Labour policies were not necessarily the same in different countries, thus raising arguable points against Anderson and his other critics—though Kavanagh was hardly meeting the main criticisms levelled against him when he also maintained that Scullin's victory did benefit the workers because it revealed to them the reactionary character of Labour when in power. (*W.W.* 20 December 1929)

But while Kavanagh and his leading associate, Jack Ryan, defended themselves in a refreshingly unrepentant way and seemingly had majority support from Australian Communists, their cause was, in the end, lost to the opposition headed by

Moxon (who had the advantage of having recently visited Russia) when a letter from the Communist International to the Australian Party was published. In this long letter the Comintern, which in the key country of Germany was currently proscribing any collaboration by the Communists with the Social Democrats against the Nazis, likewise repudiated in Australia support for the Labour Party. The Australian Communist Party, it insisted, must assert itself as a "mass party" instead of "regarding itself as a sort of adjunct to the Left Wing of the Labour Party". (*W.W.* 6 December 1929) In the upshot, this intervention from headquarters abroad was too strong to be resisted and at the Party Conference at the end of the year (which Anderson apparently attended) Moxon was made leader of the Party, with Sharkey as his lieutenant.

Anderson was thus on the winning side, and through his association with Moxon—who was the Communist with whom he had the closest contact—he was given the title of "Theoretical Adviser" and became a voice listened to in Party councils. But further developments soon followed. Kavanagh fought on and had a following in Sydney, and so a Comintern agent was sent from Moscow to clean up the Australian Party. This agent was Harry M. Wicks, who had been a leading figure in the American Communist Party, but who, when he was in Sydney in 1930–1931, went under the name of Herbert Moore. Under that name he wrote numerous articles in *The Workers' Weekly* attacking reformism and the Labour Party. In this way he undermined the position of Kavanagh, who was later expelled. In addition, however, Wicks became critical of (or could not manipulate?) the new leader, Moxon, and he too was soon demoted and later forced out of the Party, with Miles and Sharkey taking over with what was to be a long-term leadership. So far as Anderson was concerned, while for the time being he remained sympathetic to Communism, his influence was curbed, for Wicks had clashed with him over the question of how to interpret Lenin, and no doubt was disturbed by his association with Moxon; at any rate, Anderson ceased to be the Party's "Theoretical Adviser".[49]

---

[49] Wicks in the mid 1930s became an anti-Communist and that is the standpoint of his posthumous *Eclipse of October*, Chicago, Challenge Publishers, 1957. In that long book he states that he "spent more than a year in Australia, where he helped direct the job of establishing what generally was referred to as a collective leadership freed of 'rightist' influences" (p. 258), but gives no specific details. According to Fred Wells, "Right Strange for Mr Sharkey", *Nation*, 2 June 1962, when Wicks was in Sydney local Trotskyists accused him of having an anti-Communist past, and likewise the American Communist Party later claimed that he had long been an undercover anti-Communist agent!

The Freethought Society

Meanwhile in 1931 there occurred the first of the public controversies in which Anderson was the central figure. When radical
students at Sydney University, late in 1930, formed the Society
for Freethought (its name was changed to Freethought Society
in 1932) Anderson became the first and continuing president of
the Society which, for the next twenty years, was to be the principal forum for his extra-curricular addresses on social and political questions. Freethought was construed in a broad way and
took in much more than criticism of religion, as is shown by the
Society's basis adopted in March 1931: "The Society (1) recognises the primacy of science, holding that in every subject, without
exception, knowledge is gained only by observation and experiment, (2) supports the widest possible extension of knowledge of
all subjects, and (3) is therefore opposed to every form of censorship and restriction of inquiry." Then on 9 July 1931 Anderson
gave his first presidential address and, because of his allusions to
patriotism as a form of restriction on inquiry, what was also his
most famous address to the Freethought Society. No complete
or exact record of his words is extant, but he spoke to the following
effect on the topic of "Freethought And Politics":

> As is shown by the Society's basis, freethought is a positive
> thing, but it can also be expressed negatively as an attitude
> of opposition to superstition, and its connection with freedom
> of thought comes out most definitely in the opposition to
> *political* superstitions or idols. An idol is any object treated
> in such a way as to prevent or hamper discussion and
> criticism. Thus a superstitious regard for or loyalty to "the
> State" or "the Country" is a noteworthy feature of modern
> political life. But such sayings as "your King and Country
> need you" appeal to prejudice and superstition and will be
> criticised by freethinkers. War memorials too are political
> idols and the keeping up of religious ceremonies connected
> with them are merely fetishes for the purpose of blocking
> discussion. They prevent critical thinking about the charac-
> ter and conditions of the last war and thus about war and
> social relations in general. (*H.S.* 15 July 1931; *The Labor
> Daily* 15 July 1931)

> In the last war the British were not at all enthusiastic about
> it when it broke out. The Government was confronted with
> the question of making the largest number support the war
> in the shortest time, and stories were fabricated about

German atrocities in Belgium in order to make the British people become enthusiastic.

On the question of political freedom, in spite of what is called "democracy" the people have, for example, no responsibility in matters of foreign affairs. Lack of freedom is illustrated by the way in which ordinary people are liable to arrest for vagrancy, consorting or using insulting language. Such laws make it possible to arrest anyone who does not belong to the propertied class. There is lack of freedom too in the fact that public servants are prevented from expressing themselves and cannot criticise their superiors. These are all questions that should be open to discussion, and if such discussion is opposed by existing laws and constitutions then these laws and constitutions must be wrong. (*D.T.* 10 July 1931; *S.M.H.* 11 July 1931)

These comments, particularly the ones on patriotism and war memorials, evidently true though they may appear to any serious student of society, had a predictable effect on orthodox Australian opinion when they were written up in the newspapers. The day after Anderson gave his address *The Daily Telegraph* devoted part of its front page to what he said, along with a photograph of him; *The Sydney Morning Herald* gave its account the following day; the Melbourne *Argus* commented, "Professor Anderson seemed to sneer at patriotism and spoke of war memorials as idols. Some of his statements were obviously erroneous." (13 July 1931); writers of letters and editorials began to complain about his "insulting" the war dead and the like; Returned Soldiers' League branches "severely condemned" him; the Royal Empire Society "expressed its abhorrence at his remarks"; and, most publicity-producing of all, the matter was taken up in the State Parliament and by the University Senate. In Parliament the attack on Anderson was launched by the Nationalist-Country Party Opposition, a number of whose spokesmen said, in effect, that while they wished in no way to curtail free speech, nevertheless Anderson should not be free to say what he said, and the Leader of the Country Party, Mr Bruxner, moved a motion worded as follows:

That in the opinion of this House, the statements made on Thursday, 9 July, by the Professor of Philosophy of the Sydney University, namely, Professor Anderson, when speaking as president of the Free Thought Association to the effect that such terms as "the State", "the country" and "the nation" were superstitious notions; that such terms as

"your King and country need you", were appeals to pre-
judice and superstition; that war memorials were idols, and
that the keeping up of the religious celebrations connected
with them were fetishes which only served. the purpose of
mocking[50] discussion, are not in accordance with the national
sentiment of the people of this State. (*S.M.H.* 15 July 1931)

This motion was debated intermittently by Parliament over the
next two months but was never passed, owing to the fact that
the Labour Government, led by J.T. Lang, was then in power.
Meanwhile, however, the University Senate, a notoriously conservative body, held a special meeting on 20 July and passed the
following motion of censure against Anderson:

> The Senate, while asserting the principle of free speech in
> universities, and assured that Professor John Anderson in
> his class lectures has maintained due impartiality in treating
> the various topics with which he has to deal, finds that,
> when discussing the questions of patriotism, loyalty, war
> memorials, religious observances, and unconstitutional
> methods in his address delivered at the University on the
> 9th instant to a society of University students, he used
> expressions that transgress all proper limits, and for so doing
> severely censures him, and requires him to abstain from such
> utterances in future. (*S.M.H.* 21 July 1931)

But despite this censure and the attacks on him by conservative
newspapers and politicians, Anderson was also strongly supported
—by University students, by *The Labor Daily* and *The Newcastle
Morning Herald*, and by Labour members of Parliament, particularly the Minister of Education, Mr Davies.

Anderson himself, throughout the controversy, remained critical and uncompromising. Commenting on the initial Press
report of his address and the agitation against it he wrote:

> Disjointed as the report was, the comment of the Minister
> of Education shows that it would convey to any unprejudiced
> person a definite and discussable position, which, as I was
> obviously aware, is opposed to quite widely accepted views.
> But the agitation illustrates what I said not merely about
> political prejudice, but about the obscurantist function of
> the Press. It shows that sensation-mongering is an enemy

---

[50] A mistake; the correct term is "blocking".

to truth, that journalism puts issues in their least discussable form, and that its place in relation to the University (or to any body of inquiring men) is—outside. (Letter to *Honi Soit*, 16 July 1931)

The Senate had not allowed Anderson to defend himself before it, but he had submitted to the Vice-Chancellor a statement on academic freedom which was quoted with approval by Mr Davies in the Legislative Assembly:

(1) A University teacher is free to develop his subject in his own way, there being a tacit understanding that he will not use his position to force upon students' minds an uncritical acceptance of any special doctrine.

(2) University societies are free to discuss any current problem or outstanding theory of the day, participation of teachers in these societies being understood to be independent of their teaching work.

(3) The University is not committed to any views put forward in these societies, the tradition of freedom being the best guarantee that it will not be so committed. (*S.M.H.* 22 July 1931)

Anderson thus remained unrepentant. In a statement, he said that many people would think the sensation now over and the matter settled, but, he went on:

The fight for freedom of thought and speech does not stop; it goes on. I have done nothing deserving of censure. I have stood for full discussion of important questions which is an entirely academic thing to do. If I am not to oppose official views this is not free speech. And until all members of the staff have been given a list of things they are not to say, they are serving under an unstated condition. The censure, I contend, ought to be withdrawn. (*S.M.H.* 24 July 1931)

The outcome of the whole controversy was a significant victory for freedom of speech. Professors had in the past been dismissed, on other grounds, from Sydney University—Brennan and Irvine were examples—and given a different constellation of circumstances Anderson might well have been dismissed for what he said, as was demanded by some of his critics. But, owing in part to the patent objectivity of his stand, he was merely ineffectively censured, and as a result the cause of academic freedom was very considerably strengthened in Australia. University teachers were unlikely to be sacked because of their *views* in the future. There was, moreover, the consequence that Anderson himself was established, more than any other radical critical thinker Australia has had, as a public academic figure, so that thereafter he was frequently able to get some sort of public hearing for his views.

There was a revival of controversy in the following year when Anderson's 1932 presidential address, on "Freedom of Thought", together with other papers by freethinkers, was published in the first issue of *Freethought*. That journal was attacked in particular by *The Daily Telegraph* in its main front page story on Saturday, 16 July 1932. "British patriotism, religious belief and faith in the League of Nations", the paper said, "are assailed in a magazine *Freethought* produced yesterday by the Sydney University Freethought Society. This was the first issue. Whether there will be others may depend on the power of the University authorities to prevent such attacks." The *Telegraph* then went on to quote some parts of Anderson's article that it found offensive: "Upholders of freethought, of the naturalistic outlook on events must regard all supernatural and mystical explanations of things as false, and will do everything possible to prevent their being accepted." "Actually the League of Nations is only an extension of the diplomatic manoeuvring that has always gone on among the Powers . . . the suggestion that a league of militaristic nations is a force for peace is on the face of it absurd." In later comments there were calls for action against the "Freethoughters". It was stated in the Press that Crown Law authorities were reviewing the journal, and leaders of the new Nationalist-Country Party State Government made some threatening noises, but in the sequel no action of any kind was taken. Anderson, moreover, had the last word, for in the next issue of *Freethought* he subjected opinions expressed by the Premier, Mr Stevens, and the Chief Secretary, Mr Chaffey, to careful logical scrutiny. Part of what he wrote runs as follows:

> According to *The Daily Telegraph* of 16 July last, Mr Stevens said that "if the statements are disloyal as they seem to be, and destructive of principles upon which the nation has been founded and of those things which are held dear by our people, then they must be stopped, and any power the Government has will be directed to that end". *The Sun* of 19 July reports Mr Chaffey as saying that there were state-

ments in this publication which were wrong in any British community, and that "it seems to me that if the people who write in such a strain are so dissatisfied with the conditions in this country, they should pack up and get out".

The attitude expressed in these statements is obscurantist in that it implies that there are "principles" or "British" views which are above criticism, and it involves fallacy because it professes to *refute* certain political contentions, not by showing that they are false, but by suggesting that only a disaffected person would uphold them and that undesirable social effects would follow from their gaining wider support. . . .

The reference by Mr Stevens to "the principles upon which the nation has been founded" suggests that at one time these "principles" were a subject of discussion, and that a definite conclusion was arrived at. Even if that were so, it would be no reason for not discussing them again now. But it is not so; no general agreement on the political structure of society has ever been come to, and the reference to a supposed underlying agreement is merely a way of avoiding discussion of political fundamentals. . . .

A similar confusion is seen in Mr Chaffey's reference to statements that are "wrong in a British-community". Instead of a direct statement that these views are false, we are presented with the contention that no Briton would hold them and the suggestion that a person who holds them should be in some other country—in other words, we have an example of that type of evasion of the logical issue which consists in meeting an argument by directing attention to the character or situation of the person who advances it. If Mr Chaffey puts this forward as British logic, he is scarcely complimenting the British; and no serious student of biology or mathematics, for example, would accept the suggestion that he should try to discover British truths in these subjects. (OF pp. 10–11)

Later in the same year Anderson was on the receiving end of a still blunter substitute for logic on an occasion when a Communist sympathiser, E.C. Tripp (later a "Trotskyist" like Anderson), attempted to give an address on the Soviet Union, illustrated by lantern slides, in the University Union Hall. The meeting was broken up by a hostile crowd of "King and Country" undergraduates, who harassed Tripp and Anderson and later made Anderson run the gauntlet through their lines when he returned to his room off the Quadrangle. (Editorial, *Freethought* No. 2; *H.S.* 2 November 1932)

Break with Orthodox Communism

1932 was, furthermore, the year in which Anderson finally broke with the Communist Party. His disenchantment with the Party came to a head in a dispute involving *Proletariat*, theoretical organ of the pro-Communist Labour Club of Melbourne University. With the inception of *Proletariat* in April 1932, Anderson was an honoured, invited contributor and wrote articles for the first two issues on "The Working Class" and "Freedom and the Class Struggle". In these articles, which elaborated for the last time his pro-Communist theories, he again criticised reformism and the leaders of the Labour party, and agreeing with the objections levelled by Marx against Utopian Socialists, he contrasted the "philanthropic" or "goodwill" view of social change with the revolutionary view. Though granting something that, as we have seen he later stressed, namely the pluralistic point that there is in society a multiplicity of groups, he argued at this time that these are socially weak and it is only the workers as a *class* who have the class consciousness, the solidarity and the "heroic values" to revolutionise society. He also took the view that while there was a dictatorship of the proletariat in Russia, this was exercised solely against the bourgeoisie, thus reaffirming a view he had advanced earlier,[51] according to which the Soviet censorship and disfranchisement of some sections of the population could be excused on the ground that this was a temporary measure affecting only the small minority (employers, traders, and so on) who were still permitted to carry on capitalistic activities. Anderson's optimistic belief at this time that the State dictatorship was not also being exercised against the Russian *workers* appears to have derived (1) from his reliance on Lenin's own optimistic views as expressed in *State and Revolution* (written in 1917 before Lenin faced the realities of revolution) and on Stalin's later pious repetition of these views (contrary, of course, to what *he* well knew was happening); and (2) from the circumstance affecting Australian radicals generally that, apart from the fabrications and hysterical condemnations ventilated in the daily Press, virtually no news was forthcoming about developments in Russia. It is evident, then, that throughout Anderson's pro-Communist phase, his optimism about Russia and about the possibilities of revolution in other countries was based primarily on a belief, not in the State or the Party, but in the role of the

[51] Letter to the Friends of the Soviet Union, *W.W.*, 14 November 1930.

workers themselves. The working class movement, he held, was a force that could revolutionise society, not just by overthrowing capitalist oppressors, but by establishing a society that would be marked by general political freedom. That was why, he argued, "It is essential . . . to proletarian theory to reject the negative conception of freedom and to emphasise its positive character. . . . To put the matter briefly, freedom is not mere unhampered activity, but is a particular kind of activity—one which is marked by initiative and responsibility, and which is of a productive character." (FC p. 8)

Anderson was thus no ordinary intellectual fellow traveller with Communism; a conception of the working class as the class of producers on whom society depends, of their aware, active participation in social affairs, and of their concern with overall political freedom exercised *from below*, permeated his thinking; and when, moreover, we note that his position was defended by independent arguments and in a language refreshingly different from that commonly employed by Party writers, it becomes clear that Anderson's was a distinctive, morally-committed and potentially persuasive version of Communism—perhaps even the finest that has been put forward by a thinker writing in English. Some Communist sympathisers of today, on reading Anderson's material, have suggested that it was patently short-sighted of the Australian Communist Party to allow themselves to lose his support; but despite examples that may be cited of continued loyalty to the Party of some genuine thinkers—for instance, the Hungarian Lukacs—there was absolutely no way in which a man as critically-minded and opposed to servility as Anderson was could have retained sympathy for the Stalinist regime or for the local Party bureaucracy that developed in the same image.

But, turning to the details of Anderson's break with the Party, the precipitating factor was a criticism made by J.B. Miles, General Secretary of the Party, of the first issue of *Proletariat*. Anderson wrote a reply in what was seemingly a gratuitous intervention, in that Miles had singled out Anderson's contribution for praise when he wrote, "Possibly John Anderson, who deals very well with Liberalism and philanthropy in his article 'The Working Class' will deal concretely with the liberals and with the liberal errors of those who would be Communists." (*W.W.* 29 April 1932) However, what Anderson took exception to was Miles' strictures on the journal's liberalism and its free expression of divergent views. Miles, he argued, was sectarian in demanding a single line and failed to see that student and other sympathisers were best radicalised, not by "the mechanical repetition of Marxist phrases", but by being encouraged to think their way, for example, through liberalism, into the correct position. "Support can only be alienated", he ended, "if every approach is met by the complaint, 'But this is not Leninism!'." (*W.W.* 13 May 1932)

When these comments provoked, in turn, counter-criticisms by Miles, Anderson incorporated his reply to them in the third article he had been invited to write for *Proletariat*, and it was the rejection of this article that led to his break with the Party. This unusual rejection of an invited article was achieved by the use of clandestine methods. According to Professor G. Sawer, then a student and editor of *Proletariat*, he did not see Anderson's article until after it was rejected, and learnt years later that a student associated with *Proletariat*, who was a "behind the scenes fixer" for the Communist Party, "intercepted the Anderson article when it duly turned up, assisted in a Communist Censorship Board hearing on same, and concurred in the verdict—to the flames".[52] But at the time Anderson and Sawer were at cross purposes, Anderson believing that Sawer, the editor, had rejected an invited article, and Sawer that Anderson had sent his article to a Communist representative instead of to the editor; though Sawer, when he did read the article, made it clear to Anderson that, in order to avoid factionalism, he would not have published all of the article.

It is no wonder that the Party was anxious to censor Anderson's article, which was soon afterwards published by the Sydney University Freethought Society with a foreword criticising the censorship that had been exercised. For what Anderson presented was a telling critique of uncritical and illiberal Communism that might well be taken as a model by those contemporary Communist Parties which are anti-Stalinist and seek to avoid the bureaucratic-authoritarian outlook and methods of the past.

In opposition to an editorial view expressed in *The Workers' Weekly* that the workers as a class develop exclusively by their own efforts, Anderson affirmed a view presented by Lenin in *What is to be Done* (1902) about the important role some middle

---

[52] "More About Alwyn", *Nation*, 8 August 1970, p. 5. Sawer was writing about H. Alwyn Lee, who had recently died and who was the "fixer" in question. (In fact Lee and another Communist student, Charles Silver, appear to have been involved.) Lee himself was one of the writers in the first issue of *Proletariat* who was a target for Miles' criticism. Lee later left the Party and became a journalist abroad where, *inter alia*, he interviewed Trotsky.

class intellectuals, beginning with Marx and Engels, have had in helping to develop working class consciousness, and he went on to uphold the need in Australia for alliances between the workers and other social groups concerned with emancipation, including intellectual groups. The repudiation by Miles of any such co-operation, Anderson argued, was not only pedantic but also bureaucratic. Of course Communists may "criticise the other elements in a 'united front'; but this implies a reciprocal right of criticism. In the same way the right of the leadership to criticise the rank and file should be accompanied by a right of the rank and file to criticise the leadership; and the leadership shows itself no leadership at all unless it welcomes, and further develops, the criticisms that are offered." (LS p. 4) But in fact, he pointed out, whereas in 1929 the "right leadership" was defeated after two months of open discussion followed by a full Australian conference, the situation in the Party now precluded genuine discussion and criticism. There was a bureaucratic leadership which lacked confidence in the masses and, blaming individuals for its own mistakes, engaged in one sided "discussions", denunciations and expulsions—for example, he cited the distorting of the views even of so recent a leader as Moxon and the tacit denial of the fact that he *led* the Party in the new moves made in 1929. Two of Anderson's main criticisms, of Communist *bureaucracy*, and of its failure to make any advances in *philosophy*, are summed up in the following passages:

> Whatever, then, be the exact relation between leadership and spontaneity, it is obvious that a *fear* of spontaneity is a sign not of leadership, but of bureaucracy. It is this which gives rise to personal abuse ... and to the guarding of members from contamination by having any contact with those who have been expelled. This has the further effect of making it necessary to expel the latter also from "fraternal organisations", which can only make it appear to non-party members of these organisations that they are dominated by the Party. And that is only one of the methods of "teaching and leading" whereby these organisations are prevented from having any independent or spontaneous development, and become merely additional bureaux. (LS p. 6)

> One particular error in Communist theory is the distinguishing of "subjective" from objective factors in history. Recent realist philosophy has shown that mental facts are as objective as anything else. But, while the distinction

between subjective and objective does not hold, the fact of independence remains. It is on this account that, taking one movement only as objective, Communists cannot understand other movements, and take their manifestations as "subjective"—hence the indulgence in personalities, in place of informed criticism. (LS p. 7)

As against this kind of stultifying approach, he concluded, it was vital for the proletarian movement, if it was to progress, to have widespread rank and file participation, to welcome genuine theory and criticism, and to have friendly connections with other radical movements, including intellectual ones.

The publication of this article provoked Communist replies (*W.W.* 4, 11 and 25 November 1932), including the brushing off of an attempt by Anderson to reply in turn, on the ground that he was not entitled "to unlimited space in our press for anarchist freedom of discussion". These replies concentrated, not on a discussion of the key issues he had raised, but on claiming that he was a "bourgeois liberal", like countless other now forgotten professorial critics of Marxism, had made a "confession of alliance with philosophic reaction, Party renegades and disruptors", and so on, thus verifying Anderson's criticisms of Communist logic and theory. In like vein some years later, a Communist writer managed, under the heading of "The Doleful Philosopher of Trotskyism" (*W.W.* 10 September 1935), to essay a satire on a paper given by Anderson without in any way disclosing the content of the paper.

TROTSKYISM, 1933-1937

The Workers' Party

If Anderson in 1932 recognised what the local Communist Party leadership had become, it was not long before he began, belatedly, also to realise that he had been in error about the nature of the Soviet regime—though, as suggested earlier, accurate information about Soviet developments were very slow in coming to Australia and even Trotsky's opposition policies and arguments were not known in substance until years after the event. At any rate, at the beginning of 1932, in an article in which he criticised the exclusive exercise of political power by the State and its "bureaucratic functionaries" and upheld "the independence of organisations" as "the condition of political freedom", Anderson was still hopefully claiming that the latter state of affairs obtained in the Soviet Union;[53] but by the following year he had shed this illusion and become a member of the Trotskyist Workers' Party of Australia.

There had been a handful of Trotskyists in Sydney earlier, but their cause did not gain any strength until 1933 when the Workers' Party (Left Opposition) was formed. Even then, and later, it was small in numbers, but was fortified by the presence of Anderson and of a number of active ex-Communists including, for example, J. Sylvester, who had stood as a Communist candidate for Balmain in 1930, but had later been expelled for criticising the Party bureaucracy. As the outcome of a conference in Sydney in May 1933, the Workers' Party brought out a manifesto criticising Communists at home and abroad and stating the need for rank and file initiative and action, and thereafter, until the

---

[53] "Political Freedom", *Zest*, No. 1, January, 1932, pp. 7-9.

end of the decade, its publication, *The Militant*, was published regularly.

In its thirty-eight page manifesto, *The Need For a Revolutionary Leadership*, in the writing of which Anderson participated, the Workers' Party criticised the Soviet policy of "Socialism in one country" and pointed out (1) against the local Communist Party that it was concerned solely to defend the U.S.S.R. and that its machinery tended to create a special kind of bureaucrat, marked not by thought or initiative, but by blind obedience to directives from above, and (2) that this bureaucracy reflected that of the Communist International throughout whose "history there has been an overemphasis on Russian problems, and an attempt to apply Russian experience mechanically to other countries". (p. 36)

In a follow-up comment, Anderson reaffirmed the Workers' Party view that "the Communist Party itself has destroyed the possibility of building mass organisations by its sectarian approach and opportunist tactics", and with reference to replies in *The Workers' Weekly* noted that once again the main points were completely ignored. "Nothing is said about the bureaucratic methods in the Party, the expulsions, the stifling of criticism; instead, we are subjected to that feeble abuse ('this foul ulcer', 'those rats', 'those renegades', 'those snakes'), which is a sample of these methods. Nothing is said about the failure to give a militant lead—it is all settled by a quotation from Stalin."[54]

In subsequent years Anderson wrote a dozen more articles for *The Militant* (most of them under the pseudonym of "J. Baillie") in which he mainly concentrated on criticising the policies of the Communist International and the undemocratic developments in the U.S.S.R. Left-wingers all over the world at that time were particularly disturbed by the failure of German Communism— Hitler came into power at the beginning of 1933—and in analyses he made, Anderson argued that the German failure flowed basically from the policy of subordinating world revolution to the protective policy of building up Socialism in one country. But Communist theorists were anxious to shift responsibility elsewhere—that is, away from themselves and, especially, on to the German Social Democrats. In fact, however, it was the German Communist Party's own undemocratic and sectarian approach that led to its failure to act in a potentially revolutionary situation, and in the end "its right-left vacillations and its theory

[54] "Our Reply to the C.P. of A.", *The Militant*, October 1933, p. 3.

of Social-Fascism, thoroughly confused and disgusted the main body of workers", so that it was the Party itself that was "largely responsible for the Social Democrats obtaining their influence".[55] But spokesmen for the Communist International, Anderson observed, when in need, blamed the masses, never their own policies. "It is a commentary on the bureaucratic outlook of the C.I. that everything is supposed to be all right at the top and all the errors are supposed to arise lower down";[56] and on the view that the Soviet peace policy (that is, no revolution abroad so as to ensure no military attack on Russia) was giving world workers a "breathing space", he ironically observed that "No doubt the German and Austrian workers will appreciate the breathing space they have had!"[57] Likewise without credence was the Comintern view that Fascism and bourgeois democracy ("Social-Fascism") were really the same. "It is the existence of working class organisations (unions and parties) that distinguishes bourgeois democracy from 'terrorist dictatorship'; it is the breaking up of these organisations that is the leading task of the Fascist forces. But for the C.I. to recognise that would mean the abandonment of its sectarian position and the making of concessions to 'Social-Fascism'."[58]

It will be noticed that Anderson, while an opponent of reformism, was now a supporter under certain circumstances of an alliance with reformist forces, namely against Fascism. His criticism of reformism, as we have seen, was for its quietism, belief in "goodwill" and repudiation of social conflicts; hence his utter rejection of the view that co-operation, for example, with Labour Party leaders, would further the cause of revolution. But at the same time he also held from the beginning, as we have seen, that the workers could not just "go it alone" but needed support, for example, from radical intellectuals and militant workers who were not Communists. However, there was also some shift away from his 1929 position in that he now recognised that there were variations in different countries under different conditions, so that, for instance, given the dire threat of Fascism as in Germany, some co-operation with reformist forces was called for. In the light of post-1929 events it may be speculated that Anderson was premature in opposing the dominant Kavanagh group in the Australian Communist Party. They, after all, did tolerate

[55] "Germany and the Communist International", *The Militant*, February 1934, p. 4.
[56] "The Comintern Shows Its Face", *The Militant*, May 1934, p. 10.
[57] Ibid., p. 11.
[58] Ibid., p. 12.

genuine discussion and, in contrast, the later Miles–Sharkey group (1) was rigidly bureaucratic and (2) when *they* came to defend a "Popular Front" they actually advocated "a people's movement" of "the workers and the middle classes",[59] and in recommending a vote for the Labour Party in the Federal election of 1937 did so (unlike Kavanagh in 1929) in an utterly slavish and uncritical way.

In this period leading up to the "Great Purges" extraordinary lies and fabrications were being spread about by Soviet propaganda, but, despite the rebuttals by Trotsky and others at the time, and despite, for instance, Orwell's later savage satires, these lies and fabrications continued to be accepted with deep conviction by Communists and many other radicals until their falsity was traumatically disclosed by Khrushchev in 1956. So Anderson, in his Workers' Party analyses, including three articles under the heading of "The International Fabricators", was an early and independent exposer of Stalinist falsifications.

Thus, in the case of the accusations levelled against Trotsky, he showed how, in a variety of cases, by judicious quotation out of context and suppression of key passages, Trotsky's position was distorted into the opposite of what it really was; as when, for example, he was made out to be a supporter of bourgeois democracy and an opponent of the Soviet Union, without its being revealed that he, in fact, believed that country to be a workers' regime that was endangered by the Stalinist bureaucracy;[60] or when he was quoted on the weakness of the Soviet regime but with the crucial omission of a statement about his belief in world revolution.[61] Likewise, referring to the trials that followed the shooting of Kirov, Anderson noted "The intellectual degradation and the unscrupulousness of the Stalinists" and their "almost incredible falsification of documents".[62] Similarly, on assessing the evidence against Zinoviev and Kamenev he came to the following conclusion: "The only way out of this tissue of absurdities lies in recognising that Zinoviev and Co. had no connection with the terrorists and that they were simply guilty of 'undermining revolutionary security' by criticising the bureaucracy, by opposing the Stalin line."[63] Later, in commenting on their

[59] Quoted by Anderson, "Stalinists Control 'Defence of Democratic Rights Committee' ", *The Militant*, December 1935, p. 5.
[60] "The International Fabricators No. 2", *The Militant*, October 1934.
[61] "The International Fabricators No. 3", *The Militant*, April 1935.
[62] Ibid., p. 7.
[63] Ibid., p. 8.

subsequent trial and execution, he noted the patently undemocratic features of their trial which so few left-wingers could see —"the hysterical atmosphere in which the trial was conducted" and how "It is a very bad principle to condemn people on their own confessions." [64]

Australian Communists, of course, followed the Stalinist line and Anderson made thrusts at thom for this from time to time. Thus when Sharkey attempted to justify the accusations against Trotsky he took him to task too,[65] and in a general criticism said, "The attitude of the C.P. of A. to Trotskyism (as well as any kind of criticism within the movement) is precisely that of bourgeois censorship—inspired denunciations, garbled quotations, prevention of access to original sources, and (when any information whatever would be dangerous) silence." [66] He also noted ironically on more than one occasion the total inability of the local Party to offer any theories or criticisms that were not imported from abroad—for example, "Our local Stalinists, as usual, have no comment of their own to make on the situation. Theirs not to reason why!"[67]

Anderson's writings on Soviet policies and views led him to make commentaries on affairs in such countries as Germany, Russia, France and China, and among these his discussion of the latter is an interesting, unusual case in that here his analysis was in part falsified, instead of verified, by historical information that later became available. In referring to the Chinese civil war of 1934, he noted, correctly, that while China's Red Army, confronted by Chiang Kai-chek's superior forces, was obviously being forced to retreat from the south-east—and to embark on what is now known as "The Long March"—these defeats were being claimed as striking victories by Stalinist propagandists, including the Sydney ones. However, in his further analysis, Anderson took it for granted that, just as Stalin and his advisers had been responsible for the catastrophic policies that led to the defeat of the strong Communist movement in China in 1927, they were still directing affairs there. The Stalinists, he complained, were still set on a disaster course because they "assign to the peasantry not only an independent role in the revolution, but the leading role".[68] Like many other commentators, he was

---

[64] *The Newcastle Morning Herald*, 5 October 1936.
[65] "Reply to Sharkey", *The Militant*, July 1934.
[66] *The Militant*, October 1934, p. 13.
[67] *The Militant*, August 1935, p. 2.
[68] "China and Soviets, the Situation Analysed", *The Militant*, May 1935, p. 5.

thus in error (1) in not realising that the Chinese Communists were now acting to a large extent independently of Stalin's directives—and were not, for example, receiving arms from Russia—and (2) in adopting Trotsky's view (and on this point probably also Stalin's view) that the Chinese revolution could be won only by a force consisting mainly of mobilised workers on the eastern seaboard, as distinct from a predominantly peasants' movement. In fact, Mao Tse-tung proved that the latter force was indeed a viable one.

But the future of Communism at that time rested primarily with the Soviet Union and Anderson believed, with Trotsky, that Russia was still a "Workers' Republic" but one that was temporarily dominated by the autocratic Stalinist bureaucracy. Consequently he was hoping, like other Trotskyists, that this reactionary apparatus would be overthrown by the recrudescence of a genuine proletarian movement. He quoted Trotsky to this effect and in his writings and addresses—which gained him some publicity in the daily Press—he emphasised the undemocratic nature of the Soviet regime and its failure to develop the political education of the masses. The Soviet electoral system, he pointed out for example, while it was extolled as an instance of "proletarian democracy", merely serves the interests of the bureaucracy and does not advance the cause of genuine democracy, which is "the participation of the whole of the population in political activity".[69] He also noted that "the extraordinary difference between the wages of the Stakhanovite worker and those of the ordinary worker" was contrary to the aims of Socialism, as was the current state of Soviet "culture".

> How [Anderson asked] can culture spread without independence of thought, without open criticism of governmental policies, with the freedom to denounce Trotsky but not to read his works? How, in general, can culture flourish in a regime of denunciation (where informing passes as a virtue)? And how is culture compatible with the prevailing servile adulation of Stalin?[70]

In this period of the mid 1930s Anderson was, moreover, working hard on Marxist philosophy, writing two significant articles on the subject for the *A.J.P.P.* and supplementing these

---

[69] "Soviet Democracy", *The Militant*, July 1935, p. 2.
[70] "Affairs in Russia Today", radio talk on 2BL, 17 September 1936, published in *The Militant*, October 1936.

by three critical reviews of Communist books on philosophy that he published in *The Australian Highway*, the journal of the Workers' Educational Association—an organisation with which Anderson and some of his leading supporters had continuing close relations. These reviews also contained some further pointed thrusts at Stalin and Stalinist logic as the following passages illustrate:

> Not much, of course, is (or could be) quoted from Stalin himself to justify Jackson's estimate of him as the "best and greatest pupil of Lenin"; but the aphorism "Theory without practice is sterile, practice without theory is blind" (in other words, theory without practice is without practice and practice without theory is without theory), is repeated as, what it undoubtedly is, a typical stroke of the leader's political wisdom. (*A.H.* 1936 p. 192)

> The book bristles with quotations from Hegel, Marx, Engels, Lenin and Stalin; these philosophic authorities (along with Plekhanov, though in his case the references are few) are given a special section in the index. But quotations from the various "deviators" would occupy no more than three pages of the entire work, and from Trotsky, who is repeatedly criticised, not a line is quoted. Denunciation covered by vague generalities—that is the recipe for the treatment of philosophico-political error. (*A.H.* 1938 p. 13)

When in 1936 details about the new Soviet Constitution were revealed, Anderson, far from hailing it with the euphoria that many people did, noted that "it incorporated many of the features which, in Lenin's view, placed the Western democracies well behind the Soviet system". Nor, he maintained, did it show any signs of the development of the initiative of the working class "although in twenty years there should have been a development of collective responsibility". (*S.M.H.* 10 October 1936)

As this last comment suggests, Anderson was beginning to question Trotsky's thesis that Russia, despite the Stalinist bureaucracy, was still a "workers' State", and in February 1937 he came out firmly against that view in a case he put to the Workers' Party. A workers' State, he argued, requires workers' *control*, which is not true of Soviet Russia. Trotsky, moreover, did not agitate in favour of workers' democracy until as late as 1923, and, in Anderson's opinion, both Trotsky and Lenin, were open to criticism for helping to establish a monolithic system which defeated democracy in Russia and destroyed the Communist International. Lenin, though he canvassed the participation of *all* in administration, put far too much emphasis on revolution as a *break* with the past—with which was associated his dubious reliance on the professional revolutionist. As distinct from the conception of Socialism as something to be secured only in the future, Anderson argued, stress should be placed on the development of co-operative activities by the workers in the pre-revolutionary *present*.

However, a call Anderson made a little later, for the Workers' Party to see the errors of Trotskyism and reconstitute the Party on a wider basis, failed to sway members of the Party, who adhered to their previous Trotskyist position.

Freethought Activity

During his Workers' Party phase Anderson continued to be very active within the University. In the years following the controversies of 1931 and 1932, he gave a variety of further papers that were critical of established or conventional opinions, particularly when he gave his annual presidential address to the Freethought Society, but also when he spoke under other University auspices, including those of the Literary Society to which he often gave papers (for example, on Joyce, Kipling, Shaw, Dostoevsky) that had social content, and those of the Sydney branch of the A.A.P.P. whose members were interested in social issues as well as philosophy. Some key examples of these papers are as follows.

In 1934 he discussed Bakunin's *God and The State* and, combining a criticism of censorship with one of religion, deplored the fact that only a censored version of the pamphlet had been permitted to appear. Later he gave an address on "Fascism" in which he argued in substance thus:

> Although Fascism pretended to be above classes, this was not so, for as long as capitalists and employees existed the doctrine of an impartial State was untenable. The chief difference between Fascism and capitalist "democracy" lay not in the absence of parliaments, for even Fascist countries have mock-elections, but in thorough-going suppression of such social activities as trade unions, and the replacing of them with institutions subordinate to the State. . . . The German workers were subdued by Hitler only because the parties which should have acted in their interests failed to take advantage of the position. . . . Fascism was really one

of the methods used by the capitalists to take back the concessions that had been wrung from them by the workers. If Fascism was not necessary here it was only because the ruling class had gained what it wanted by fraud rather than by force. (*H.S.* 4 July 1934)

His presidential address to the Freethought Society in 1935 was on "Censorship", and in view of the important place criticism of that government action has in his social thought, a report of that address is also worth quoting at length:

The three lines along which censorship operated, sedition, obscenity and blasphemy, were more closely connected than would appear.

The obsession with sex would not be cured by censorship, which encouraged it, but by education. It was no use pretending that the banning of pornographic literature would protect people of "immature" mind, since life itself cannot be censored. Furthermore, the assumption by the governing class of moral guardianship over "immature" minds was illogical, since those protected were nevertheless supposed to be adult enough to elect their moral guardians into office. In a democracy the citizens should be regarded as responsible beings.

Religious censorship destroyed the scientific attitude by making people unwilling to investigate on their own account. It led to the idea of the "sin" of sex, but what was needed was more freethinking and responsible living in matters of sex.

Censorship of literature for religious and sexual reasons really reverted to political issues, for the governing class was aware that people who think freely on religious matters will also think freely on political matters; it was the latter that they feared.

Censorship was moreover essentially undemocratic; it was the working class that suffered most from censorship. (*H.S.* 1 May 1935)

In 1936 his presidential address on "Social Service", later published in *Freethought*, No. 3, set out his criticisms of philanthropy, and in another address on "Censorship" he emphasised the contrast between democracy, the active and responsible participation of citizens in political life, and the censorious approach, which suits governments because it keeps the masses docile and unquestioning. Then in 1937, in his presidential address on "Censorship and Monarchy", he dealt with the issue of the day, the abdication of Edward VIII. Criticising the censorship and deception practised by the British Press in its reporting of the event, he went on to comment generally on the anti-free-thinking character of social symbols and ceremonials. Symbols such as a king or a flag, he argued for example, by "covering over actual conflicts and the rapacity of prominent leaders and organisers, support a misleading solidarist view of society, which plays into the hands of plutocratic propagandists". (*U.R.* 15 April 1937) Later in a discussion on "Australian Literature", he criticised the demand for literature of that kind and the view that there is good literature that is peculiarly Australian. "There is no more an Australian literature", he said, "than there is an Australian philosophy or an Australian school of mathematics. Australians should contribute to the literature of the world." (*H.S.* 13 October 1937)

Anderson rounded off his growing disillusionment with Trotskyism in an address to the Freethought Society. Speaking on "Why Bolshevism Failed", he repeated some of the criticisms he had voiced to the Workers' Party but developed others as well. Trotsky, he argued, did not go back far enough in his own criticisms, for this would have involved him in a criticism of his own past and his adherence to Leninism. In Russia there was an arbitrary and tyrannical system, but the origins of the system lay in Leninism, in its fundamental belief in the Party, and its failure to develop workers' control. But "Trotsky believed in the Party as much as his present opponents did; even in 1926 and 1927, when he was dissatisfied with the policy of the Communist Party and regarded the Party itself as a sham, he made no appeal to the workers at large." (*U.R.* 30 September 1937) Of course, the origins of the Party and its conspiratorial character were connected with the Tsarist autocracy, but that did not alter the extreme narrowness displayed by Lenin—who assumed that he and the Party alone knew what was in the interest of the working class. "This attitude, connected with the intellectual superiority of Lenin, tended to drive away all able men besides Lenin (Trotsky is an example, though he became reconciled with Lenin at the time of the revolution), leaving in the Party those who were fit only to be followers." (*U.R.* 30 September 1937) The police and indeed gangsterist character of the present regime "can be traced back to the early Bolshevik Party, for example to the way in which it was financed by banditry under the name of expropriation. The attitude of fanaticism, that the end justifies any means, can be seen even in Trotsky's action in putting down the Kronstadt rising. . . . It is this attitude that saps the sense of justice and in the end justifies any atrocity." (*U.R.* 30 September 1937) What was needed, he argued, was a return to Marx's conception of the new society growing within the old, for the workers must begin to develop an appropriate way of life under capitalism itself if they are ever to take over the running of society.

FREETHOUGHT AND THE
EXPOSURE OF ILLUSIONS,
1939–1949

Concentration on Freethought

With the further trials in Russia and the developments in Spain during the Civil War, Anderson became still more disillusioned about the prospects for Socialism when, in 1938, he was away on sabbatical leave. He spent his leave mainly in Scotland though he did also visit Oxford and New York. In the latter city he saw Max Eastman, whose book, *Marx, Lenin and the Science of Revolution*, had had some influence on him and whose political history had a parallel with Anderson's own, as Eastman had been an early and leading American pro-Bolshevik, then an admirer and translator of Trotsky, but subsequently had become disillusioned with Trotskyism as well.[71]

After 1937 Anderson ceased to be a supporter of the Workers' Party and when he returned to Australia he took his criticism still further by giving a paper to the A.A.P.P. in Melbourne on "Socialism" in which he now questioned the fundamental parts of Marx's own position. He did, however, remain on more amicable terms with members of the Workers' Party than he

---

[71] Eastman was at that time under attack from American Trotskyists, notably James Burnham and Max Schachtman. Later when Anderson was criticised in *The Militant* (June 1939) for abandoning Bolshevism, that journal stated that a more than ample reply to his kind of position had just been given by Schachtman and Burnham. But these two men themselves repudiated Trotskyism within the year—which incidentally shows that Anderson was an independent thinker and a forerunner in his 1937 thinking, and once more different from the numerous Australian radicals who are so dependent on overseas sources for their ideas.

had with the Communists after his break with them. While Anderson was abroad in 1938 some of his supporters started up a new group, the Democratic Group, which "set out to study and extend democracy" and tried at first "to recruit from a wide variety of disciplines—economics, law, etc." [72] The Group ran for a couple of years with Anderson taking part in its discussions on his return. Effectively, however, the Workers' Party was the last would-be popular, and the last working class movement with which he was associated. From now on, though he continued to speak out publicly on many issues, a segment of the University population was to be the base for his political activities and the Freethought Society the principal place for the expression of his socio-political views. These views, also, were to undergo some change as he now began to refine them into his position of permanent opposition to dominant authoritarian forces and the servile outlook they engender, and the related exposure of prevalent social illusions.

In 1939 the Freethought Society heard him speak presidentially on "Totalitarianism", when he reflected on the question, If Bolshevism has failed, why has Fascism succeeded? Part of the answer he went on to give was that the Russian regime had become steadily more totalitarian, so that there was a considerable parallel between Russia and Nazi Germany, in that the State and Party were all-powerful in each case and political freedom was denied. It was, moreover, false to maintain, as the Communist International had done, that Fascism was merely a capitalist device, for it was plain that Fascism interfered with capitalism in certain ways. But he concluded that totalitarian regimes based on the use of force could never entirely prevail, and may in the end themselves break down, because of the inescapable fact of social *pluralism*. In the same year, it is interesting to remark, he had Enoch Powell, then the University's Professor of Greek and an ally of his on the question of classicism, speak to the A.A.P.P. on the subject of "Nietzsche on Education".

On the outbreak of war in September 1939 and thereafter most Sydney academics, as in the previous war, were dutifully patriotic—for example, one of Anderson's professorial colleagues became Chief Censor for N.S.W. with two other professors among his assistants. It is thus safe to judge that Anderson, the antithesis of an uncritical chauvinist, was not warmly regarded by the University establishment, particularly when he continued

---

[72] Letter from W.H.C. Eddy to A.J. Baker, 24 July 1963.

throughout the war to advance disturbingly unorthodox views. However, he also had considerable support within the University during the wartime period; apart from the loyalty of his lecturers and students, there was the fact that a forceful Student Senator of this time (F.W. Fowler) was sympathetic to him, as were a series of editors of *Honi Soit* in the period 1941–1945.

It was an old issue that came up in 1940 in a dispute concerning the Freethought Society—the question of an open platform. Some opponents of Anderson had sought to have some staff members with different views elected to the Society's Committee, but Anderson had prevented this on the ground, as he later wrote, that membership of the Society was open only to those who accepted the Society's platform, the basis of which was that it "upholds secularism and opposes all forms of censorship, maintaining that no exact meaning can be attached to the notions of 'sedition', 'blasphemy' and 'obscenity' and that all legal proceedings on the basis of such notions are inequitable". (Letter to *Honi Soit* 15 May 1940) This was reminiscent of an earlier, more formidable attempt that had been made by University Christians, in 1931, to infiltrate and capture control of the Society, in response to which Anderson and other freethinkers had placed a veto on membership by non-freethinkers. Anderson had at that time made some apt comments that are worth reproducing:

> There is nothing either in freethought or in freedom of thought to imply a welcoming of all views or the setting up of an open platform. . . .
> The supposition of the emergence of truth from the pooling of all views is one which would occur only to those who do not sharply distinguish the true from the false, and who therefore cannot expect us to take their theory seriously. The assertion that truth is found to lie between extremes of opinion depends on mere vagueness as to the meaning of an "extreme" view. To say that a certain view is held only by a minority, even a fanatical minority of persons is to say nothing against its truth. And if there is a definite clash of opinion on a specific issue (if, for example, we have the views that freedom of thought is good and that freedom of thought is not good), then there is nothing whatever between the "extremes". We may, of course, suspend our judgement on the particular issue, but there is nothing scientific about suspension of judgement; it is merely a confession of ignorance. . . .
> The plain fact is that there is nothing a view can be except

true or false, and that certain views are irreconcilable with certain others. . . . (FT pp. 1–2)

In his presidential address of that year, on "The Present Position of the Labour Movement", Anderson criticised Labour's meliorist concern with minor reforms within the system, sympathised with Sorel's syndicalist opposition to political parties, and spent some time analysing the social strata involved in the Labour movement. The left-wing unions, he noted, while usually narrowly concerned with wages and conditions and having little interest in political theory, do reflect in an instinctive way genuine rank and file militancy. But, by and large, he argued, the Labour movement is not confined to workers but appeals to the discontented of *all* strata, including those people without an outlet for their talents. From these usually come the Labour lawyers, parliamentarians and union leaders who, while not necessarily consciously hypocritical, do form a stratum that profits from the situation. These people are parasitic on the Labour movement in that without that movement their jobs would not be available for them.

In 1941 his presidential paper to freethinkers was on a quite different topic, "Liberal Education". That view of education was one he had long defended against authoritarian and utilitarian conceptions and he was to defend it again and again for the remainder of his life, in reaction to the pressures that increasingly came to be exerted on schools and universities. "Education", he said, criticising the N.S.W. Department of Education, "must not be confused with specialised training. Education involves training for participation in social and political activity. It involves the encouraging of initiative and criticism. But training in criticism leads to criticism of the very institutions in which one is working, and the demand by Ministers that teachers should not criticise educational institutions is just a demand that they shouldn't act as educated men or, ultimately, as educators." (*H.S.* 15 May 1941)

A little later, in a symposium on religion, he was heard making one of his recurrent comparisons, that between Christianity and Communism, when he compared "the credulity of the Evangelical Union with that of the Russophiles, who are equally dependent on testimony and accept, credulously, doctrinaire versions of the conflicting testimony of certain trials". (*H.S.* 14 August 1941) Then, in September, when the Federal Government's ban on James Joyce's *Ulysses* was re-affirmed, Anderson spoke at a large Literary Society meeting which unanimously passed a motion demanding an immediate withdrawal of the ban, and he followed this up with a powerful article he wrote for the A.J.P.P. on "Art and Morality". Some of his typical arguments in the article run as follows:

> The supporters of the ban on *Ulysses* assume that their conception of morality is one that all must accept. Their position would obviously be weakened if they admitted that they were speaking only in the name of *a* morality, if they had to uphold what we may call the morality of protection against the morality of freedom.... (AM p. 253)

> Just as "the only check that ought to be placed on literature is criticism" (A.R. Orage), so good literature is itself critical and revealing, and protective literature, the literature of comfort and consolation, is bad.... (p. 255)

> The best intentions in the world will not succeed by such methods in *bringing about* equality, in bringing the lower orders up to a higher level; it is by what they *are*, not by what they are given, that men will win release from servitude.... (pp. 258–59)

> Actually, *Ulysses* would produce little or no effect on the immature; it is a book for the mature, but not for the servile, who are shocked by it because it confronts them with a freedom they have lost, because they can no longer face unpleasant facts and particularly their own defeats, because it attacks the ceremonial and fetishistic system by which they conceal these things from themselves.... (p. 261)

The article also interestingly presents some of his sexual theory:

> Is the position, then, that sexual freedom has a particular secularising tendency, that it cuts more sharply than other "transgressions" across the hierarchical system? It is certain that, in moralistic theories, hierarchical conceptions are most strikingly applied to sexuality; thus it is demanded that sexual enjoyment be subordinated to reproduction, and the independent pursuit of it is regarded as a grievous sin. In fact, it is especially in regard to sexuality that the conception of sin finds application and "guilt" is felt; and it may be that, without exercising some command over the sexual life of the lower orders, authorities could never keep them docile.... (p. 261)

1942 and 1943 were dour years during the war with Japan, but the activities of the Freethought and Literary Societies were kept going and Anderson also wrote two of his most original ethical and social papers, delivering to the A.A.P.P. and then publishing, in 1942 "The Meaning of Good", and in 1943 the particularly influential "The Servile State". In the latter article Anderson expressed disquiet about the curtailment of liberty and the decline of culture (not in the "bourgeois" sense but in the sense of independent, productive cultural movements) that (1) were occurring through the regimentation associated with the war effort and (2) would, he feared, be accentuated by post-war plans to bring about "security" and "welfare". The "welfare State" and its attendant planning bodies, he argued, would in fact promote servility, regimentation and a low level of culture. His article ends with a memorable statement of the case for *struggling for freedom*:

> How far the process of social regimentation and cultural degeneration will go it is, I think, impossible to say. What can be said is that so long as there are rights of opposition (so long, for example, as we are not subjected to a one-party system) culture will still have a front to fight on. And here independent institutions are of special importance—institutions, that is, which are not merely nominally autonomous but have a *doctrine* of independence; Universities, trade unions, and the like, which will resist being treated as servants of the State, or in which, at the worst, a resistant minority will remain. For the measure of freedom in any community is the extent of opposition to the ruling order, of criticism of the ruling ideas; and belief in established freedom, or in State-guaranteed "benefits", is a mark of the abandonment of liberty. The servile State is the unopposed State. (S p. 339)

Criticisms of Religion

During these war years Anderson was also active in criticising Christianity, within the University and in general. In one striking formulation he argued against a University critic as follows:

> Christianity has a certain general character as Feuerbach showed, its principle is subjectivity, whereas the principle

of philosophy is objectivity. It does not matter from which side criticism begins—with the philosophic criticism of the notion of "dependent existence" and of a "scheme of things" or with the ethical criticism of philanthropy. The outlook in either case is a servile one. . . .

When, at the Arts Symposium, I said that Christianity should be "attacked", I took the expression from the *Honi Soit* report I was quoting. My main point was that University students should be acquainted with the case against Christianity, the case for secularism in general (which is a philosophic case) and the special case against Christian ethics —and, I would add, against "constructive programmes and mutual appreciation of viewpoints". When I said that the University was cluttered up with "believers" I meant with people who had safeguarded themselves in advance against learning anything, who with the object of "saving their dirty souls" (the phrase, is, I believe, Matthew Arnold's) rushed straight into organisations for maintaining their old outlook and gave the University no chance to overturn it—who thus treated the University as a mere means to a living. Modernistic Christianity does it all in a more refined manner; it may give fancy interpretations to "fatherhood" and "sonhood" and all the rest of it, but it cannot get away from personalism and dependence, that is, from servility —only a secularist philosophy can do that. . . . (Letter to *Honi Soit* 2 July 1942)

Then in 1943 the second famous public controversy occurred in which Anderson was involved. The New Education Fellowship, a Sydney body, organised a series of five lectures on "Religion in Education" which were given by various clerics and educators, including Anderson, the others of whom advanced predictably conventional or compromise opinions on the subject. Anderson, however, on 1 April, was forthright in stating and arguing for his view that "As with the subject of snakes in Iceland—one could say, 'There is no religion in education'" (RE p. 25), and when his lecture was reported in the daily Press there was an enormous outcry up and down the land. Writers of letters to the Press compared him, for example, to Hitler; blasphemy was mentioned in Sunday sermons; he was publicly cursed by a clergyman in South Australia; the Minister of Works and later Premier, J.J. Cahill, expressed interest in having Anderson prosecuted; he was condemned by Parliament; and, in general, there was a public dispute that went on for weeks.

Proponents of authoritarian religion and morality have long claimed for their doctrines a privileged position in Australian society and it is only in quite recent times that their hold on the community has weakened, so it is not surprising that they were vociferous in their opposition to Anderson, for what he presented was a considered, emphatic statement of the secularist position. In summary, he maintained that education is the development of inquiry and habits of investigation, but religion is opposed to education because it sets up limits·to inquiry by introducing notions like the "sacred", which are precluded from examination and are supposed not to be open to observation and experiment. Consider, for example, the assertion that God made everything and the child's response to this: "But who made God?" "In asking this question", Anderson commented, "the child is proceeding sensibly; he is using the conception of 'making', to which he can give a meaning in terms of his own experience, in order to bring the conception of God within his grasp. But when he is told that God is uncreated, that is something which he cannot bring to the same test." (RE pp. 25–26) Like other religious dogmas, he went on, such a conception is an attack on the child's commonsense. The inculcation of religious dogma, he argued further, is inimical to education in general because it encourages either a cynical pretence to believe or else a credulous, submissive outlook. The latter outlook, which carries over into other fields and helps to promote political servility, is engendered, in particular, by religious teaching to the effect that God is an all-powerful policeman whose authoritarian demands the child cannot dodge. But, in fact, Anderson argued, despite its religious cover, the authority concerned is always a human and arbitrary one:

> We may be told that the author of all things wants us to act in this or that way, for example, to be chaste. But how can it be proved that he prefers chastity to unchastity? His "representatives" will tell us that the injunction to be chaste is found in his sacred word. But how can they show that word is his, what ways he has of communicating with human beings? The decision must be made quite arbitrarily—just as arbitrarily as it is decided that certain events happening nearly two thousand years ago (I am not here concerned with the question how far the Gospel narratives are historical) give a better clue to the nature of things, are a better embodiment of ultimate authority, than any other events

we like to take. We are always brought back to some human fiat; the authorities to which we are asked to submit are earthly ones. (RE p. 27)

In the remainder of his lecture he upheld the secularist approach to all subjects, and maintained that subjects like history, as much as religion, should be taught in a "controversial" as distinct from a dogmatic, uncritical way. He granted that there were worse enemies of education than religion—for example, wartime patriotism and the whole utilitarian approach to education—but nevertheless held that the Christian ethic stood low in the scale of moralities. It did have features of some value, namely, its sense of human limitations as against cheap "scientific" optimism, and its opposition to revengefulness—though he noted that the divines in wartime were silent on that subject—but even so these matters were best dealt with in a secular way. His conclusion was that religion, as a subject of education, needed to be treated as part of the general history of culture, though in that case it would be essentially a subject for study by adults rather than by children.

In the sequel, the official outcome of the controversy was the exact reverse of that in 1931 when Anderson had been censured by the University Senate but not by Parliament. For now the Legislative Assembly, with abstentions but no negative votes, passed a motion against him that ran as follows:

(1) That, in the opinion of this House, certain statements relative to religion and education made by Professor John Anderson, Professor of Philosophy, Sydney University, in the course of an address to the New Education Fellowship on 1 April 1943, and subsequently published in the Press are unjustified, inasmuch as they present a travesty of the Christian religion and are calculated to to undermine the principles which constitute a Christian State.

(2) That the terms of this resolution be remitted by Mr Speaker to the Senate of the University of Sydney.[73]

The University Senate, however, supported Anderson and in the reply it gave to the Legislative Assembly pointed out that the University Act lays it down that "no religious test shall be applied to the teachers or the students of the University", and said further,

---

[73] Quoted in the Appendix to *Religion In Education* (five addresses) brought out by the New Education Fellowship, 1943.

"remembering, as it does, the results that have followed the regimentation of universities in other parts of the world, it is also strongly of the opinion that nothing but harm would follow the stifling in the University of the spirit of free inquiry".[74] Anderson, moreover, received considerable public support. Within the University various student societies, including the Evangelical Union and the Students' Christian Movement, defended his freedom of speech, and he received support in the downtown Press, particularly in *The Daily Telegraph*—compare for example, its leader under the heading of "A Witch Hunt in A.D. 1943", 7 April. Anderson himself remained critical and uncompromising, and with reference to the Legislative Assembly attack was quoted as saying that members of the Assembly were as ignorant of his lecturing work as they were of the argumentative character of the address they criticised. (*S.M.H.* 7 April 1943) Speaking in the Philosophy Room on 21 April at what was perhaps the most crowded meeting the Freethought Society ever held, he spoke to the following effect:

> If free discussion does offend some people then they must be offended.
> The theorist cannot recognise any limitation of freedom of speech and academic freedom, and has the right to be as blasphemous, obscene and seditious as he likes, whatever offence may be sustained by vested interests. In practice certain restrictions may have to be observed, but not in ways which would prevent the consideration of theories. The question is therefore one of the degree of academic freedom to defy Government decrees, such as the ban on *Ulysses*, or on the discussion of revolutionary Socialism.
> Academic free speech would in time encourage free public speech in general. There were, for instance, strong interests in the State trying to prevent free discussion on sex. If a man overrides these restrictions, his treatment of sex will simply be dismissed as "revolting". Instruction in venereal diseases usually takes the form of telling young people "not to" and rarely consists in critically presenting the facts.
> The issue of religion was one of the many cases where the support and freedom of the Press was essential. (*H.S.* 29 April 1943)

As in 1931, the outcome of this more widely publicised controversy in 1943 was that Anderson had distinctly furthered the

---

[74] Ibid.

cause of freedom of speech. Thereafter religious authoritarians were muted in their attempts to silence critics of his kind.

Criticisms of Communism

In the following month (May 1943) there was another public controversy, though this time of much smaller dimensions, that partly involved Anderson, the antagonists on this occasion being the Communists. P.H. Partridge, a Philosophy lecturer at the University, who had studied under Anderson and was a member of his "school", had written a course of lectures for the Workers' Educational Association in which he was critical of the Soviet Union and argued that it was in no sense a workers' State. This had occurred in October 1942 and had led to a conflict with the Communists who sought, unsuccessfully, to have the course withdrawn. But there was a public flare-up in May 1943 when it was announced that the N.S.W. Trades and Labour Council had cancelled its affiliation with the W.E.A. because of Partridge's course, and he became a target for attack by Communists and left-wing sympathisers generally. Partridge, however, spoke out in defence of his position, as did Anderson and other freethinkers, and the result was the unusual expression—in wartime 1943 when patriotic enthusiasm about the Soviet army was at its height—of forceful criticism of Russia for the totalitarian character of its regime. Communists, however, returned to the attack in 1944 when, for example, a Communist spokesman offered as a substitute for a reply to what Partridge actually said the comment that "Trotsky was a Fascist and that Partridge was a Trotskyiter"! (*H.S.* 6 April 1944)

In 1944 it became apparent that the war would be won by Russia and the Western democracies, and Anderson, when he gave a series of Freethought papers on "Trotsky" in second term, took the opportunity to sum up his views on Communism—and, in commenting on post-war problems, to criticise the assumption made by the Allied side that there was just *one* enemy of peace in Europe (Germany), and to come out with the unpopular-with-patriots, but indisputably pluralist, view that the best outcome of the war would be a *negotiated* peace.[75]

In his appraisal of Trotsky, Anderson re-traversed some of the ground he had covered in his 1937 papers but he also made

---

[75] Compare also his short article, "Check Imperialism", in *The Daily Telegraph*, 14 April 1943.

various additional points. Trotsky, he argued, had contributed as much as anyone to the dictation of opinion inside Russia and to the suppression of the opposition, and it was here, in their suppression of the opposition, including bourgeois parties, that the initial error of the Bolsheviks lay, an error that he went on to trace back to the triumph of the undemocratic line taken by Lenin in the original split with the Mensheviks in 1903. Apropos "Lenin's Testament", Anderson held that while this contained no very clear analysis, it did suggest, not that Lenin wanted Stalin replaced by Trotsky, but by someone else who was more adaptable and honest than Stalin. On Lenin he argued further (in line with other, especially more recent, analysts) that it was his methods of organisation that enabled Stalin to get into power. It was not that Lenin had made any valuable contribution to general social theory; what he did contribute was something that proved to be most damaging to the cause of genuine revolution, namely, the theory of the authoritarian party and the accompanying conception of the professional revolutionary—which was another conception that Trotsky did not oppose. In another of his observations, Anderson deplored the habit people now had of identifying with Russia questions about Socialism and revolution and their consequent ignoring of the insights of pre-Bolshevik thinkers. He also spoke at length on the Spanish Civil War, expressing a view independent of, but not dissimilar to, that, for example, of George Orwell. Thus the anarchists and the P.O.U.M. in Spain, he held, were genuine fighters for the cause—though the Stalinists tried to spread all manner of lies about them—and there was a genuine attempt at revolution in Catalonia when there was an armed seizure of the factories and the large estates. But the belated intervention of Soviet Russia, by denying arms to the anarchists and by introducing into Spain G.P.U. agents and their methods of execution and assassination, had led to the crushing of the non-Stalinist working class forces and ensured the triumph of Franco. Anderson also drew attention to the incredible blindness of English liberals who, he said, though they could see through the tyrannies of Hitler and Mussolini, were quite unable to see anything wrong with Soviet Russia.

Post-War Activities

With the end of the war in 1945 came a new phase of University life. The student population was considerably enlarged and Anderson continued to be very active in extra-curricular affairs, occupying himself for the rest of the decade particularly with questions about censorship, education, Communism and the Labour Government.

In the middle of 1945 there was a public controversy over *Honi Soit*. In that year, freethinkers were closely associated with its publication. When an issue of the paper was brought out containing articles under such headings as "Pox Vobiscum", "Mattress Music", "In the Beginning Was the Word and the Word Was Odd", that criticised and satirised current religious and sexual views, there was an outcry, especially by Roman Catholics, and the University Senate sought unsuccessfully to have the *Honi Soit* editor sacked. Anderson, of course, was quick to repudiate such an attempt to interfere with freedom of criticism and wrote cuttingly about the attitude of the University authorities: "After the vigorous discussion provoked by the issue of *Honi Soit* of 12 July, the Senate's pronouncements come as a dismal anti-climax. Apparently it is beneath the Senate's dignity to argue the point, to specify the 'objectionable' parts of the published material and to show what is the precise objection to them. But it is not beneath its dignity to exercise mere authority and to ignore the findings of the students' elected representatives." (*H.S.* 13 September 1945)

Three years later more material in *Honi Soit* was regarded as "blasphemous" and "obscene" and this time the Senate intervened over the head of the Student Council and banned the paper for a time. Anderson, though he was politically antipathetic to the 1948 editors of *Honi Soit*, was again quick to defend students' rights—indeed, it was noted at the time that hardly had the Senate's ban become known around the University before Anderson was addressing a Freethought Society meeting called to protest against it. This time he wrote up his views in an independent student paper brought out during the ban. As with other rights, he argued, students' rights are best maintained by "active citizenship", for example, by participating in University societies or airing views in student publications. Their education, moreover, may even be aided by ribaldry, for that customary feature of student life may help to break down bonds, including the bonds of "good taste", that may restrict their thinking. "Students", he went on, "have the right to be criticised and to meet that criticism openly; they have the right not to be badgered, not to have standards forced on them but to develop their own standards."[76]

[76]"Students' Rights", *Heresy*, 12 May 1948.

That view of student intellectual life was a reflection of his overall view of the Faculty of Arts in University education. In 1945, for example, he criticised the tendency towards Government control of universities on the ground that it was inimical to education and "profitable only to vested interests and managerial careerists", and argued that a strong Faculty of Arts was needed to counteract related tendencies of a professionalising and commercialising kind.

> It has been argued against me in the past, [he wrote], that Arts studies as a whole do not encourage a critical mentality. But at the very least it can be said that they are less professionalised than those of the other faculties. And it may be added that they do in general operate against provincialism of time and of place, that they make the student conversant with a body of literature from which he can get a sense of the contributions of various nations to culture and the folly of adherence to merely local values. (*H.S.* 15 March 1945)

Meanwhile, in the more narrowly political field, he continued his criticisms of left-wing forces in Australia, objecting, for instance, to the "utilitarianism" and "jobbery" characteristic of both the Labour and Communist Parties, and noting that while the latter Party was attractive to students because it was opposed to "repressive and intimidatory forces such as the Returned Soldiers' League", the fact was that Communists themselves employed the very same methods. (*H.S.* 17 March 1949) As for the Labour Party, this was the period of the post-war Chifley Labour Government with its "planning" and its extending bureaucracy, contemporary opposition to which is illustrated by the lines of the Sydney poet Harry Hooton:

> We hated the "bloated capitalist" once
> And his "blackleg, scabbing rat",
> We fall for his smug successor now,
> The Labor bureaucrat.[77]

Anderson made references to Labour in his chief Freethought address in 1948 on "Progress and Reaction", in which he argued that no matter who are in charge of a ruling system, they are reactionary and opposed to free and critical thinking in science and in the Arts. The so-called "progressives", he went on, are wrong in their view that it is a matter of improving material

---

[77] "The Perfect State", *It is Great to be Alive*, published by M. Elliott for the Twenty-First Century Art Group, Sydney, 1961.

conditions first and then, second, of attending to the spiritual side, for the latter would be lost while concentrating on material betterment. Thus the Labour movement was nominally concerned to promote equality, including equality of culture for those who are at present deprived of culture. But, he argued (here re-affirming his early view that the workers need to *learn* from the best intellectual and artistic elements in bourgeois culture), the trouble is that the deprived classes with their existing outlook and habits, that is, with their existing lack of culture, are themselves supposed to be the instruments or determinants of cultural improvement, and under these circumstances there will be reaction, not progress, and true culture will degenerate. Labour, he allowed, can do useful work as a critical opposition, but is a failure when in power, partly because it entails the tackling of problems by people who lack any sense of tradition. Its educational policies, he argued in conclusion, are particularly bad, as they emphasise utility as against disinterested inquiry and make the "progressive" assumption that what is "the latest is the best". (*H.S.* 18 March 1948)

Anderson, however, was quite even-handed when it came to dispensing criticism, and the next year someone of a more conservative complexion was the subject for a Freethought Society paper. This was the newspaper proprietor, Warwick Fairfax, who had devoted to Anderson one of his weekly newspaper columns and mentioned him in another.[78] Fairfax in some literate but not very profound speculations, said of the Freethought Society that it "apparently forbids us to believe in a singleness of purpose in the universe", referred to the question of "good manners" when dealing with controversial matters, and to Anderson's disbelief in religion, and the like. The upshot was an address at which Anderson examined Fairfax's observations and objected, in particular, to the "anti-critical" and "external" view of education he adopted in drawing a protective distinction between controversial and non-controversial subjects and in suggesting, for example, that parents had a choice between sending their children to study under the religious disbeliever, Professor Anderson of Sydney, and the believer, Professor Gibson of Melbourne. In a follow-up Freethought meeting, Anderson complained about a misleading report on the first meeting in *The Sydney Morning Herald*, and took the opportunity to criticise generally the inaccuracy of newspaper reporting, and pointed out that the only accurate

[78] "Casual Converse", *The Sunday Herald*, 27 March and 3 April 1949.

reports of his addresses over the years had been those reports in *Honi Soit* that he himself had prepared. (*H.S.* 28 April 1949)

It was in this decade, 1939–1949, then, that Anderson came to sponsor freethought as a tough-minded position concerned to expose illusions and to oppose the servility-promoting forces that abound in society, whether their complexion is "conservative" and bourgeois, or "progressive" and proletarian. In his view, the cause of freedom, criticism and cultural achievement was one carried on essentially by resistant, trans-class minorities, for the one potential candidate in modern history for bringing about an overall regeneration of society, the working class, had plainly failed to live up to the hopes that had been placed in it. It was because of his view that workers in the mass were interested, not in revolution, but in "security", and were prepared to tolerate despotism to have it, that Anderson refused when, in 1946, former Trotskyist associates made overtures to him to take part in a revival of the old political activities. He now regarded as much sounder the view of Max Nomad that in revolutions old rulers are merely replaced by new ones and that the correct policy is one of perennial opposition.

This position of perennial or perpetual opposition (Nomad also called it "permanent protest"), which Anderson re-affirmed in a Workers' Educational Association course in 1947, did not represent any really sharp break in his thought, for in his theory of ethics, as we have seen, he always took the view that *good* will be a minority force, and with reference to the permanence of criticism he was much earlier on record as saying:

> A life spent in philosophy is a life of struggle, of struggle against problems, a struggle for knowledge against forces of error and ignorance, which were particularly strong in this society, and might perhaps exist in any possible society. Thus intellectual struggle is a course which arises in demands in opposition to obscurantism, but the demands do not remove the evils, and only the existence of definite social forces can sustain the struggle.[79]

What he had done, however, was to hone his always critical freethought approach into a position that was fundamentally one of uncompromising criticism and opposition on all fronts. Consider, as a detailed illustration, which also reveals his talent for making topical connections, the report of one of the finest

[79] A.A.P.P. address on "Philosophy and Life", *Honi Soit*, 21 June 1933.

addresses he ever gave on "Freethought", his presidential address in 1945:

> He began by saying the Society had consistently opposed censorship and rejected the conceptions in terms of which censorship was commonly exercised. But while it thus stood for freedom of thought, for the public presentation of all views including what is now called "Fascism", it had a specific doctrine of its own, freethought, which was quite misinterpreted as the "open platform". Freethinking had been specially associated with opposition to religion, but that characterisation was inadequate. It was opposed to all forms of superstition, and thus to the belief of "rationalists" in a fundamental reality and in constant human progress. This sort of evolutionism was an example of "ideology", that is, it was concerned with comfort more than with truth, with "practical" more than with theoretical considerations. The optimism which did not see that there would never be a "rational" society, and that freethinkers would always be a minority and an opposition, was not itself freethinking. The religious person believed that things must ultimately be well, and the rationalist adopted the same position, merely substituting Nature or Evolution for God.
>
> Freethought was concerned, then, with the critical analysis of current superstitions—of all systems of consolation, protection or salvation—in short, of popular morality. When people gave thanks for the success of British arms, they were not in general thinking of God as a combatant who had entered the lists at particular times and produced particular results. But in that case was their thanksgiving any more than an expression of group solidarity, a recognition of the fact that by that solidarity they had maintained their possessions and crushed a formidable rival? Assuming that religion had such a content, freethought was concerned to uncover that content and to reject the tribal morality of possessiveness or acquisitiveness.
>
> But as against the view of many rationalists, the solution was not to pass from the solidarity of special groups to world solidarity. Anything that passed as such would be marked by the same acquisitiveness as the special groups exhibited. The nations professing to be establishing world security now gave no signs of relinquishing their privileges or abating their powers—Britain of freeing India, America of giving social equality to Negroes, Russia of abandoning State-dictated justice and State-imposed opinion. The belief in collective security was just another superstition, helpful only to those in possession.

The freethinking position was one of opposition—opposition to the setting up of idols and to the search for security. In its struggle with the idol-worshipping mass freethought sometimes made advances and sometimes suffered setbacks. It was at a low ebb during the present war, when the utterance of the word "Fascist" was thought to settle all political questions—a situation for which we were bound to suffer politically in the period to come. But there would always be some who questioned accepted values, and freethinking views had a greater chance of survival in a cultural tradition, than consolatory doctrines which could be picked up at any time. At present the daily Press and, to a large extent, the system of popular education were powerful breeders of confusion. But it was the natural condition of freethought to encounter such difficulties and to face up to them. (*H.S.* 17 May 1945)

ANTI-COMMUNISM, EDUCATION
AND ACADEMIC FREEDOM,
1950–1962

The next stage in Anderson's development was marked less by a definite change in his overall thinking than it was by an alteration of emphasis and interest. While he continued to speak out forcefully and critically on social issues, he now tended to concentrate on certain recurrent themes, notably on Communism and its dangers and, as part of his unwavering defence of disinterested intellectual inquiry, on anti-educational developments within the universities. He was also involved, towards the end of his life, in further public controversies in the course of which he vigorously championed the cause of academic freedom.

Anti-Communism and Freethought Conflicts

Anderson, as we have seen, had long criticised Communism for its monolithic character and its obliteration, in any country in which it seized power, of freedom of thought and criticism, but his preoccupation with it to the exclusion of other political topics—particularly in the "Cold War" period of the early 1950s—was a new development that first began to manifest itself on the occasion of the Australian coal strike of 1949. That strike was largely engineered by the Communist Party—under the influence of its then leader, Sharkey, who has since been criticised by some Communists for his "adventurist tactics". When Prime Minister Chifley sent troops to the coalfields to break the strike Anderson voiced support for him, thus appearing to go against his standard pro-democratic pluralist view that trade unions and their exercise of the right to strike provided a vital check on the power of the bureaucratic State. However, what he suggested was not just a crushing of the coal strike but provision for an "organisational outcome" that would lead to the formation of "alternative unions"—which, presumably, would be characterised by workers' democracy instead of Communist manipulation. (Letter to *Honi Soit* 13 July 1949)

In the late 1940s the question of banning the Communist Party (which had been banned in 1940–1941) began to be aired widely, and Anderson, in a discussion of the subject, combined a repudiation of Communism with a succinct statement of the case against such a ban. The suppression of a particular political view, he argued, even if a government is empowered to do so by a popular referendum, is undemocratic because it is not an exercise in effective citizenship on the part of the people, but a passive handing over to a privileged minority of the power of guardianship. As he put it in one of his formulations:

It is idle to say that the Communists themselves suppress opposition views wherever they can. Of course they do; all supporters of dictatorship do. But if that were a reason for following their example, dictatorship would have won. The view that "we must fight the enemy with his own weapons" was a common one during the last and the preceding war; but what is maintained by undemocratic means is not democracy but some special interest. The mark of democracy is publicity, is the open discussion of issues, is the open statement and refutation of all varieties of *undemocratic* opinion—Communism, Fascism or what you will. In fact, the policy of driving certain positions out of the political arena plays into the hands of the Communists in that it implies that there are no general principles of political liberty, that the question is only "Who is to dominate whom?" (PP pp. 7–8)

But by 1950, when Menzies introduced a bill to ban the Communist Party, Anderson, while opposing it, was somewhat more emphatic in his opposition to Communism.

It may be [he told freethinkers] that the Menzies bill is a bad one, and anti-democratic. But the Communists themselves are perfectly unscrupulous, and capable of any underhand action. Any attack on Menzies' proposals should

be accompanied by an attack on Communism. . . . It is
always a question of whether things haven't already gone
too far; whether we are confronted by a choice of tyrants,
and whether our political freedom has so decayed that
tyranny is inevitable. I cannot pronounce on this; but there
is no comparison between the tyranny of Communism and
the repression that may be introduced by Menzies. (*H.S.*
4 May 1950)

Then in the following year, after the bill had been disallowed
by the High Court, the Menzies Government sought to have the
ban upheld by a referendum (in which, in the sequel, the No
vote won, largely owing to the spirited campaign of Dr Evatt).
On this occasion Anderson, while still not endorsing the ban,
fell out with many of his supporters, owing to his refusal to have
a paper given to the Freethought Society in defence of the
No case.

A conflict within freethinking ranks had already arisen over
the question of military conscription. When that measure was
introduced by the Menzies Government in 1950, in an objection
to it a body of students at Sydney University, many of whom were
freethought sympathisers, formed an Anti-Conscription Committee. Then, in a surprising move, Anderson criticised their
stand in an address at a large Freethought Society meeting which
was also remarkable for the fact that at discussion time none of
the other speakers supported him. The view he advanced was
that "To be political is to have a power of deciding on what
front we are going to fight—to have a sense of what is an
immediate and important issue", but compared with the major
issue of the encroachment of Russia and proletarian ideology,
the issue of conscription was of slight importance. (*H.S.* 7 September 1950) This statement appeared to go against the earlier
freethought conception of "fighting on all fronts", by which was
meant exposing illusions or struggling against illiberal tendencies
wherever they manifest themselves. In his address he also spoke
about armies, saying "it was possible for there to be democratic
armies: the Australian Army for example in the First World War
had the reputation of being a democratic army" (ibid.), thus
echoing a view he had presented some years before on "Servility
and War" when he had distinguished between bodies of soldiers
with greater and less disfranchisement or servility, though at
that time he had displayed no sympathy for conscription and
had stressed the importance of *volunteer* armies. (*H.S.* 3 July 1947)
In a further comment on the student Anti-Conscription Com-

mittee, he criticised the attitude to it of the community and of the University authorities (who refused to recognise the A.C.C. as a University society) and defended the Committee's "right to be wrong", but reiterated his view that the fundamental political stand should be one of opposition to Communism.

> I do not, indeed, deny [he wrote] that there are widespread political superstitions in "democratic" societies and that exposure of them will show incidentally that they have something in common with those current in "proletarian" societies. The fact remains that proletarian superstition is the disease of our time, and that no "exposure" which does not treat it as central is of any effect. (*H.S.* 21 September 1950)

In 1951 Anderson was confronted for the first time by a Freethought Society committee a majority of which opposed him on some issues, and various conflicts occurred in the course of that year including, as mentioned above, conflicts over the Anti-Communist Referendum, and, in particular, over the question of sexual theory. On the latter question, Anderson and other freethinkers had in the past often criticised conventional sexual moralism, accepted Freudian views about the repression of sexuality, and pointed to a connection between sexual freedom and political freedom. But, despite this and despite, for instance, an earlier observation that "you cannot remove customary restrictions *in thinking* without removing other restrictions as well",[80] Anderson now seemed anxious to disclaim any suggestion of sexual radicalism. It was not altogether clear whether he agreed with some among his remaining adherents who went so far as to maintain that freethought was solely concerned with exposing illusions and thus had no interest whatever in policies, including any policy of seeking to promote social or mental conditions that might assist people to see through prevalent illusions. But he was certainly displeased with "Libertarian" freethinkers when, on the question of sexuality, they claimed that a way of behaving which included an active sexual life might help students to liberate themselves from their sexual illusions, and he appeared to have this view as a target when, in an address on "Freethought" in October 1951, he rejected the suggestion that there could be any linking of freethought views with particular activities or particular ways of living. The exact character of Anderson's views

---

[80] "Students' Rights", *Heresy*, 12 May 1948.

in these disputes was obscured because of a penchant he now had, which was partly an expression of his sense of satire, for stating his opponents' views in an exaggerated form. Thus, on the general question of the "Libertarianism" of his recalcitrant followers, he attributed to them a crude, freedom-from-constraint point of view when in a paper on "James Joyce" he spoke, for example, about the need to emphasise "the importance of the positive, creative character of freethinking and the illusion involved in the attempt to lead the untrammelled life, the negative attitude of disbelief traditionally called Libertarianism". (*H.S.* 20 September 1951) Likewise on sexual questions, he imputed to his opponents naive advocacy, for instance, of what Freud called "wild analysis", that is, of trying to solve people's problems by merely telling them to go and have sexual intercourse, which was hardly a fair rendering of the socio-sexual position, partly influenced by his own writings, that they were advancing.

If Anderson did not at that time present any specific sexual theories of his own, he had done so in the past. One is the theory that has already been mentioned, which he put forward in "Art and Morality" when he suggested that there is a connection between sexual servitude and political servitude. This view which, perhaps, he wished to disown in 1951, has obvious affinities, for example, with some of Wilhelm Reich's views on the subject and is one that influenced Libertarian freethinkers. Another of Anderson's theories, which he had developed at greater length, relates directly to the question of overcoming sexual illusions. In a paper on "Obscenity",[81] Anderson largely followed Freud and Ferenczi in treating the explosive and contemptuous force of "obscene" words as an expression of distorted sexuality that is connected with the retention in adult life of feelings associated with the stages of infantile sexuality. Then, referring to the Freudian view of the two attitudes to woman that are commonly and ambivalently exhibited, namely, a treatment of her on the one hand as a sentimentalised "virgin mother" and on the other hand as a degraded "prostitute mother", he noted that there is a parallel distinction among types of copulation between the senti-mental-subservient and the brutal-dominant. In neither of these cases of brutality and sentimentality, he went on to argue in an original way, is there a free and equal exchange between the partners in the sexual act and, indeed, owing to the anatomical

---

[81] Read to a Freethought Society study group on 28 October 1940, and circulated in typescript, over the years, among freethinkers.

differences between the sexes, it is impossible for copulation, on a phallic basis, to be an act of equals. However, if we take account of the theory that the comic is the exposure of illusions,[82] there is a possible way in which both the sentimental and brutal approaches would be avoided and sexual equality achieved. This is by "comic copulation", that is, by the partners having an outlook of such a kind that the *phallic* or *potency* illusion is seen through.

The disputes of 1950 and 1951 were the culmination of a growing lack of rapport between Anderson and some of his potential student followers. He retained his "charisma" in the lecture room and continued, for the rest of his career, to attract able and dedicated students who went on to major in philosophy, but there was some estrangement between him and the wider class of socially-awakened students who had normally been receptive to his ideas. This was partly because of changes brought on by the influx of ex-servicemen and other students after the war, not a few of whom were brasher and less respectful towards learning than formerly, and whom he tended to distrust on principle as illiberal "leftists"—sometimes with good reason, for, for example, it is now known that at least one of the editors of *Honi Soit* in the late 1940s was at the time an undercover Communist. But there was also, on Anderson's side, the effect of his own political history, his deep disillusionment over Communism and over the spread of a "servile, welfare-State" mentality, which made him fear that society generally was perhaps on the verge of "a new age of barbarism". Consequently, he himself became less patient and more inflexible, and hit out at once at any vocal students, including students attached to him and his views, if he suspected that they were at all being taken in by "proletarian illusions". Perhaps, too, he was hurt that what he had to say could no longer command the immediate acceptance it formerly had done.

All the same, this re-orientation of his approach was very much a matter of his concentration on certain themes rather than others, and of the vehemence with which he was often heard voicing his criticisms. So far as his general theory of society was concerned this remained largely unaltered. He did not write much on that subject in subsequent years, but what he did write —including an important summation of his views on Marx in 1959 (RA)—was consonant with his earlier writings, which is

[82] In Anderson's view of dramatic literature, it is in comedy, as distinct from tragedy, that there can be a thorough exposure of human illusions. Compare his "The Comic", *Hermes*, Journal of the University of Sydney, 1936, pp. 10–12.

why, in Part I, his social philosophy has been set out as a single position.

After 1951 the Freethought Society became defunct, for in later years Anderson made no attempt to revive the Society, preferring, if need be, to address an improvised student meeting, while a number of the other freethinkers, for their part, founded the Libertarian Society which, though disclaimed by Anderson, continued, to a considerable extent, to give voice to his theories. He himself continued to take an active part in University discussions of public issues—except during a year of study leave in 1953, which he elected to spend at home in Sydney working on his philosophy—and from time to time kept up his criticisms of both "popular" and "establishment" illusions.

After the death of Stalin and the subsequent "thaw" in Russia he became less preoccupied with Communism, though this remained one of his principal targets for attack, along with censorship, religion, welfarism, egalitarian education, and the general direction in which Australian political parties were moving. At one time, in opposition to the post-war Australian Labour Government, he had canvassed the recrudescence of a genuine *liberal* Liberal Party concerned with the "exposure of bureaucracy and 'government by regulation'" and freed from its ties with the "narrow interests" and "narrow views" of the Country Party. (PP p. 12) Even then, however, his hopes had been slight, and when the Liberals were again in power he did not find them advancing causes he favoured, such as developing the political education of the electorate or seeking to reverse that breaking down of traditions and barriers which "has encouraged the growth of a class of professional paid politicians—and, therewith, improvisation in the increasing number of fields in which it interferes". (DI p. 17)

Educational Issues

Above all, Anderson reanimadverted upon the growing decline of education, particularly at the university level. Upholders of cultural values, he argued, instead of shrinking from public controversy, must be prepared "to attack progressivist and egalitarian dogma and to uphold privilege", for unless tertiary institutions retained their traditional independent and privileged status, learning and criticism might well be drowned by the utilitarian and other anti-theoretical forces that abound in the community. (DI p. 18) That view appeared in print in 1954 but was, of course, of no avail, for within a space of four years his worst fears began to be fulfilled with the advent of the Menzies inspired Murray Report on Australian universities. Anderson at once, prophetically, commented that the price of the recommended large expansion in "the national interest" would be loss of independence by the universities and a dilution of university studies by treating them as if they were of the same kind as secondary school subjects. As against the "co-ordination" and "planning" envisaged by the Report he argued as follows:

> Any overlapping and wastage which does occur is not to be set against the independence of the universities in the advancement of subjects. The alarm at the high failure rate assumes that universities are mere training centres for the professions, and shows concern with pushing students through in the minimum of time rather than being concerned with presenting students with problems about which they are to think critically.[83]

In a later, scathing attack, he pointed out that the new policies were largely being imposed on universities by people who were uninterested in scholarship and investigation.

> University teachers in general [he wrote] are more and more taking on the character of coaches and ushers, concerned with getting students through ("eliminating wastage", as the phrase goes) and not with finding out who is capable of rising, under a certain intellectual stimulus, to a certain intellectual standard—a standard which can only be aped, not attained, by those who have been given "personal assistance", and shown the methods of passing. (PA p. 5)

He also criticised the influential Association of University Teachers for its lack of interest in truly academic matters and its overriding concern instead with salary increases, and went on to give a characteristic magisterial survey of the state of academic life as follows:

> But we have to take a pluralist view of the University as well as of society in general and to see that, within any

[83] Report by D. J. Ivison of A.A.P. meeting on "Education", Sydney Libertarian *Broadsheet*, No. 3, May 1958.

so-called academic institution, there are non-academic and
anti-academic activities—that what is academic (for it is
a question of movements and traditions, and not of "individuals") has to fight for survival against pseudo-academic
Philistinism as well as against the incult social mass, that
the struggle of culture against "bourgeois society" exists
also on the campus.

   This has always been the case; but the academic had more
of a fighting chance when any member of staff might be
assumed to have had a liberal education in which he
acquired some knowledge of the classics of literature and
philosophy. The absence of that condition today explains
the absence of any distinctive and recognised academic view
of public affairs; its place is taken by the naive and unlettered
views which emanate not merely from scientists but from
psychologists and educationists. It would be especially on
education that strong academic pronouncements would be
looked for, but the baleful influence of "the new education"
has ensured that University spokesmen are commonly as
devoted to philanthropy, as concerned with aids to careers,
as the most ignorant outsider. In view of all this it could
almost be said (although critical voices are still raised here
and there) that the place of the *academic* in modern society
is nowhere. At any rate, while it may be of interest to
consider how the academic spirit will, where it survives,
express itself, it is clear that the voices that speak in the
name of the universities are, for the most part, far from
academic. (PA p. 5)

   Men who publicly endorse fine principles all too often forget
them in practice, so it is worth remarking that Anderson in his
own academic conduct largely lived up to the spirit of his criticisms. With his Scottish background of learning and his devotion
to critical inquiry he was remarkably immune from the power-
seeking and patronage-concerned motives that so much infect
Australian academic life. He was incapable of interest in rising
in the University bureaucracy, he would not even become Dean of
the Faculty although he had an unsurpassed knowledge of the
regulations, and he was so free from an omnipresent kind of
imperialism that he actually did not seek additions to his staff.
In University appointments, moreover, he stood trenchantly for
use of academic criteria alone. For example, in one notable case
in the early 1950s (which did not become public knowledge), a
University selection committee, of which Anderson was a member, nominated for an Arts chair a man whose critical and

scholarly work plainly put him in first place. But sharp practices were employed, involving a distorted accusation of sexual impropriety against the nominee, and in the sequel, though Anderson fought tooth and nail on the issue, the appointment of the selected man was overruled.

Anderson's cause was thus always the cause of intellectual inquiry and that was why he opposed pressures for university expansion and for large salary increases; he sought to preserve universities as small but independent institutions which, bourgeois and philistine though they were in various ways, were still centres in which learning had at least a prominent place, and he foresaw that with expansion, outside interference would increase, administrators would become more powerful, and above all, inquiry and criticism would decline.

More Public Controversies

Meanwhile the much publicised Orr Case had occurred, in which Anderson took a prominent part. Sometimes referred to as the Australian "Dreyfus Case", this concerned what was believed by many people to be the "framing" of Sydney Sparkes Orr, Professor of Philosophy in the University of Tasmania, because of his political opposition to the reigning University authorities.[84] There had been considerable staff discontent at that University, and in October 1954 Orr expressed criticisms in an Open Letter· to the Premier and Minister of Education. The upshot was a Royal Commission in 1955 whose findings supported many of the criticisms made by Orr and other members of staff, but allowed the existing University authorities to remain in power. Then in March 1956 Orr was summarily dismissed from his post by the University Council on the basis of four charges, the main one being a charge that he had been guilty of sexual misconduct with one of his students. Orr brought an action for wrongful dismissal to the Tasmanian Supreme Court but the judge found against him on the crucial sexual misconduct allegations, and the High Court of Australia declined to reverse this judgement. There ensued a public controversy that went on for a decade and in the course of which Anderson, like his colleague, Professor A.K. Stout, was an early and unremitting defender of Orr. Through

[84] For full details of the charges and evidence, and a powerful exoneration of Orr, see W.H.C. Eddy, *Orr*, Brisbane, Jacaranda Publishers, 1961.

their example and efforts, funds were raised in Sydney in 1957 to help pay for Orr's appeal to the High Court, and they took a leading role in the exchanges of opinion which led in 1958 to a majority of professional philosophers in Australia and New Zealand declaring a "black ban" on the appointment of a successor to Orr by the University of Tasmania. It was only in 1966, by which time Orr (like Anderson) had died, that a compromise settlement was finally negotiated with the University and the ban lifted.

What Anderson contributed to the Orr Case, in addition to his support for Orr personally, was a careful scrutiny of the general issues involved and in consequence an emphatic defence of academic freedom. He was concerned (1) to criticise, as Orr had done, the "master-servant" conception of the relation between universities and their staffs, (2) to deplore the comparative slowness of the Association of University Teachers and academics generally, apart from the philosophers, to realise the issues involved and to rally to Orr's defence, and above all (3) to insist, as in the following passage, on the principle of academic and sexual freedom for university teachers:

> Professor Orr's answer to the question whether a professor who seduced one of his students should be dismissed—"Yes, of course, he should"—seems to me while it is understandable enough, to confuse the issues. Presumably the suggestion of "seduced" would be that the action in question related to the conduct of the professor's department; and it will be remembered that, while Mr Justice Green thought it obvious that any such relations would affect a professor's academic integrity, no evidence was offered that Professor Orr's work as a teacher had been affected by his relations to any student.
>
> ... I suggest that no proof is possible which would not involve other charges of flagrant misconduct and neglect of duty. More broadly, it can be said that (to take a phrase from Professor Orr's "agitational letter") "students are not children" and that the personal relations of either staff or students are not the University's concern. What ensures high University standards is enthusiasm for learning; and no one has ever been able to question Professor Orr's devotion to his subject and to his educational work.[85]

Moreover, in advocating greater public spirit on the part of University teachers who, he held, all too frequently acquiesce

[85] "The Orr Case and Academic Freedom", *The Observer*, 28 June 1958.

in the direction of their affairs by "worldlings", Anderson praised Orr's original stand in criticising the Tasmanian University authorities. Orr, he maintained, in "breaking through the reconciliatory pretences" was someone who "fulfilled the requirements of an academic position immensely better than the mass of Australian 'academics'". (PA p. 5)

Anderson had retired from his University post at the end of 1958, but continued to speak out on issues that affected the universities. Then, a year before he died came the last important public controversy in which he was involved. This concerned Dr H.R. Gough, Anglican Archbishop of Sydney, and to a lesser extent a Roman Catholic, Dr V.J. Kinsella—two gentlemen whom, it turned out, atheists would no doubt have been pleased to invent if they had not existed. When Archbishop Gough, in a sermon to a legal gathering on 6 July 1961, came out with a denunciation of University philosophers for advocating Communism and free love, what he said immediately made headlines in all the newspapers and continued to do so for some time afterwards.

> The world today [the Archbishop was reported as saying] faced a grave threat from the teaching of Marxist Communism. The basic philosophy of Marxist Communism is that there is no God. In place of the Deity there is the State, a master to whom unquestioning obedience is necessary. Here in Sydney we have those who are shamelessly teaching in our universities these same soul-destroying philosophies. I am not saying that such lecturers are Communists. But they are teaching ideas which are breaking down the restraints of conscience, decrying the institution of marriage, urging our students to pre-marital sexual experience, advocating free love and the right of self-expression. Evidence of this kind is even now before the N.S.W. Advisory Youth Policy Committee. . . . (*D.T.* 7 July 1961)

It soon emerged that he had also been inspired by a pamphlet written by Dr Kinsella, who was a retired medical specialist. This pamphlet, *Empiricism and Freedom*, referring at length to Anderson, assailed him for his empirical philosophy that contains "the seeds of moral corruption and political subversion", and made various comments about Communism and Nazism and what happens when unwholesome ideas are allowed to spread. As any trained philosopher could see at a glance, Kinsella's arguments were at a low level and were accompanied by such observations as "rubbish", "this naive, cheap and low-minded philosophy", "the young man and girl, holding hands and dreaming of marriage and home together, demand above all else from each other that they be clean and faithful"; and he must have been something of an embarrassment to his church, for its spokesmen did not rush in to defend him and his pamphlet had earlier been criticised by the Roman Catholic Chaplain at Sydney University.[86] Gough, however, had been seemingly impressed, and Anderson was accordingly forthright in his counter-attack. "It's a disgrace", he was quoted as saying, "that a person like Dr Gough couldn't see straight away that Dr Kinsella's pamphlet is illiterate stuff. The pamphlet is not on an intellectual plane at all; no one could take it seriously." (*D.T.* 8 July 1961) In the case of Gough, Anderson expressed doubts about whether he had any knowledge of philosophy or Communism—justifiably so, it appeared, in the light of the Archbishop's not very intellectual credentials[87]—and went on to deny flatly Gough's charges and to uphold freedom of discussion of all subjects including sexual ones:

> Unless different theories can be expounded and discussed there can be no progress. It's no use having to ask the Archbishop's opinion every time you want to suggest a new theory. In my thirty-two years at Sydney University, I never heard a Philosophy teacher advocate free love or pre-marital experience in the lecture-room. What he expresses in private is his own business and not the Archbishop's or Dr Kinsella's. (*The Sun* 7 July 1961)

Gough was widely criticised, in the ensuing public discussion, for his wild and censorious charges, and Anderson followed up at a lunchtime meeting of students on 14 July with what proved to be his last address at the University. In a memorable performance, he vigorously attacked attempts to interfere with University autonomy and freedom of speech, and captured the attention and the imagination of the very large audience when he said:

> If there was a charge of the *corruption of the youth* by University teaching, one could compare the position with that of Socrates who, having given a life time to the study of what was corruption and what was improvement (or education)

---

[86] Letter to the Editor by (Rev.) Roger Pryke, *The Catholic Weekly*, 7 May 1959.
[87] Compare *Nation*, 15 July 1961, for an account of Gough's academic background and general outlook.

was confronted by accusers who, as he was able to show, had carried out no such study.[88]

On moral questions, he pointed out, he himself in fact upheld an *objective* ethics, though it was very different from the ethics of obligation advanced by Christians, whose own activities were not "of a high moral level". He then re-affirmed his standard criticism of religion for its "*personal* view of reality" and "the fairy tales" that it promulgates, and ended with a call on University people to resist clerical encroachments:

> The immediate occasion of the present controversy should remind us of the constant endeavour of the clerical forces to encroach on work which is essentially secular and which, more particularly, is marked by a rigour which clerics cannot approach. Any success in such encroachment would lower the intellectual level of University life and *ipso facto* lower its *moral* level to a greater extent than could be done by anything the ranks of piety complain of, even where it is not a mere fabrication.[89]

John Anderson reached the age of sixty-eight on 1 November 1961. He died on the following 6 July.

Appropriately, the last public comment he had made for the Press was on an issue concerning censorship. The Department of Prisons had refused a prisoner in Goulburn Gaol permission to read books on philosophy and psychology, and although another professor was quoted as supporting the prison officials' stand, Anderson, of course, came out firmly in favour of the prisoner's freedom to read. "For some prisoners", he commented, "the subject would be very suitable. I definitely don't think any person should be barred from studying philosophy. You don't know if the people who banned these books know the content of the subjects. I think their only reason could be ignorance." (*D.T.* 21 March 1962)

---

[88] "Academic Autonomy and Religion", *Honi Soit*, 27 July 1961.
[89] Ibid.

EPILOGUE

What has been the impact of Anderson's social thought since his death? The answer is that, despite the force and range of his work, his influence has been surprisingly little. The roll call of old "Andersonians"—if we use that term very loosely—indeed remains a most impressive one, embracing some fifty or more University professors and lecturers, in philosophy and a number of other subjects, and in addition numerous people in a variety of other influential occupations, including in particular, law. But while quite a few of these ex-students of Anderson have no doubt continued to be attached to his social doctrines, the ironical fact is that it is through the activities of some isolated individuals rather than through the medium of an intellectual or social *movement* that his theories and policies have been kept alive. Thus, even in general philosophy there has been no real continuation of Anderson's thought except in the teaching of four or five philosophers scattered among several universities. But in the area of academic social philosophy his work has been neglected still more, and so far as Anderson-inspired movements of the Free-thought Society kind are concerned, the only later comparable movement was that associated with the Libertarian Society at Sydney University, which functioned from 1952 until 1969 and whose members, *inter alia*, combined Anderson's pluralist social theory with Nomad's notion of permanent opposition.

In the last few years, however, there has been a tendency to *mythologise* about Anderson by identifying his views with those of a certain group of "Andersonians" who have been notable for supporting American policies in Vietnam and some of whom have been associated with the conservative journal *Quadrant*. It is this casting of Anderson in a thorough-going conservative or "right-wing" mould, moreover, which has probably contributed to the neglect of his work by more radically-minded contemporary students and scholars. Now, apropos Anderson personally, it is true that he was subject to a "hardening of the categories" in his last years so that if he were alive today he might possibly have come to have the overall position of these conservative "Andersonians", though it is also quite possible that, ever intransigently critical in his outlook, he would have repudiated them and their views—compare the fact that Anderson in his lifetime, when confronted by the pronouncements of some of his followers, was wont to retort, echoing Marx's comment on Marxists, "I am not an Andersonian".

These, however, are merely loose conjectures about how a man might have reacted in old age. If we attend instead to more solid evidence we can reject the attempt to fasten posthumously on to Anderson the extreme political views of his alleged followers.[90] For one thing, the claim to be "Andersonian" of most members of the conservative group in question has a quite tenuous basis, and few of them had sympathy for Anderson, or his views, when he was alive. For example, one telling piece of evidence is the fact that in the Orr Case conflict—which, as I have narrated, occupied Anderson in his last years—a number of the *Quadrant* "Andersonians" were firmly anti-Orr. But the crucial issues concern the views Anderson held and here, as was brought out earlier, what he did *write* in his last years is quite in accord with the social position he advanced in his maturity. Thus, he did go on criticising the "welfare State" for its passive, servility-inducing conception of citizenship and for its promotion of covert managerial and bureaucratic interests, but he did so in the cause of defending rank and file democracy and, generally, the activities he described as *good*. Moreover, he was no simple anti-Marxist and retained to the end much respect for Marx's contribution to social theory. Nor, when he complained about the "acquisitive" and "consumerist" outlook of the mass of the workers, did he wish to exempt capitalists from his strictures; unlike some contemporary campaigners against Communism and against the "welfare State" he was in no sense a spokesman for big business.

Suppose we do, in the light of his actual writings, speculate on the application of Anderson's views to, for example, present

[90] Compare my comments in *The Australian Journal of Politics and History*, December 1976, pp. 445–47.

day Australian politics; it is then easy to see that none of the leading protagonists escapes censure. Thus, the Whitlam Labour Government is of course open to sharp criticism for its jobbery and nepotism and, above all, for its naive "hoping for the best", social "planning". But the Liberal Party dominated governments before and after are likewise open to condemnation because, notwithstanding their ideological rhetoric about "freedom" and the like, they have done nothing to promote democratic and non-servile values, and have merely exercised government from above while cultivating the myth that they too can successfully "plan" for "the needs" of society. On the subject of Anderson's conception of non-bureaucratic government from below, that, indeed, is not something that has been furthered by any of the dominant parties, *or* by the powerful directorate of the Australian Council of Trade Unions. Amongst established organisations it has been, remarkably, the Communist Party of Australia which —despite its continued adherence, in the main, to doctrines of the kind criticised by Anderson—has at all concerned itself with supporting rank and file participatory democracy as, for example, occurred when its members were prominent in the Builders Labourers' Federation. Furthermore, on the controversial issue of the action of Governor-General Kerr when, owing in part to Opposition control of the Senate, he intervened and dismissed the Whitlam Government, the Andersonian viewpoint is arguably one of opposition to Kerr's intervention. For although Anderson regarded the electoral process as merely a secondary feature of democracy, opposition to actions of the Kerr kind is suggested, for instance, by the following typical statement of Anderson's position: "Democracy ... is misconceived as a mere electoral mechanism—a mechanism on which, in any event, Upper Houses and other agencies of delay and veto are superimposed. Only that system is democratic in which the people are politically active, not merely at election times, but all the time, and in all institutions." (*H.S.* 18 July 1934)

Although, then, Anderson's influence in recent times has been slight, what he presented is a powerful and potentially revivable position, with regard both to social theory and social practice. As against bourgeois social theorists who remain very much wedded to atomistic and solidarist notions, and as against Marxist and other radical theorists who advance a half-fledged view of social conflicts according to which pluralist society will in the end obligingly become solidarist, Anderson offers a thorough-going pluralist theory of the working of social forces, and as such a theory that is deserving of careful study and development. Similarly, on the side of supporting or promoting the cause of political and intellectual freedom, he offers a position, alternative to the usual ones, that could again become attractive at least to realistic minds. For, as against the simple "white versus black" and "final solution" conceptions of social issues that abound among fashionable "rightists" and fashionable "radicals", Anderson draws attention to disturbing complexities. Freedom, he holds, is only *one* social force among many, and it is not an end or a reward that is to be finally achieved in some utopian future; it is a positive form of social activity with its own ways of going on, here and now. Freedom, moreover, is something that has to struggle for its existence, and part of its constant struggle is against prevailing illiberal forces and prevailing illusions, wherever they are found.

INDEX